D0563199

ENGRAVING GLASS

A BEGINNER'S GUIDE

BOYD GRAHAM

DOVER PUBLICATIONS, INC., New York

This book is dedicated to Eddie

This Dover edition, first published in 1991, is an unabridged and slightly corrected republication of the work originally published by the Van Nostrand Reinhold Company, New York, 1982. The color plates, which originally formed an insert, have been repositioned on the covers for the Dover edition.

Library of Congress Cataloging-in-Publication Data

Graham, Boyd.
    Engraving glass : a beginner's guide / by Boyd Graham.
        p.   cm.
    Reprint. Originally published: New York : Van Nostrand Reinhold, 1982.
    Includes index.
    ISBN 0-486-26683-4 (pbk.)
    1. Glass engraving.   I. Title.
[TT298.G7 1991]
748.6—dc20   90-21460
                                                        CIP

Manufactured in the United States by Courier Corporation
26683405
www.doverpublications.com

Acknowledgments

A very special thanks to my wife, Eddie, for her help in making this book possible through her encouragement, typing, editing, and moral support, and, in general, for getting the job done.

My appreciation to my children, family, and friends for their support and thoughtfulness toward my glass engraving endeavors. A special thanks to those who gave permission to reproduce their engraved glass in this book. My gratitude to Nancy Robinson and Juanita Zachry for their literary advice, and to editors Nancy Green, Leslie Wenger, and Irene Demchyshyn for their interest, help, and patience. And finally, to those who in any way had a hand in producing this book.

Contents

PREFACE

The first time I saw an exhibit of Steuben engraved glass I was spellbound. It was difficult to believe that people actually, physically, carved those beautifully enchanting designs into hard glass. The impression was of ethereal figures suspended in air and framed with shimmering light. I had to know more about it. I began an enthusiastic, extensive search for books, pictures, and information concerning the exquisite art of glass engraving. There were a few books available with black-and-white as well as color reproductions of finished glass engraving, but very little information existed on what process was used to accomplish the finished product.

Several years passed, but my fascination with engraved glass did not diminish. I was determined to learn how to do it. From information gathered, I soon decided that the cost of copperwheel engraving equipment and knowledge of its use were beyond me, so I had to take a different approach.

I first tried abrasive grinding wheels with a small handheld motor without success. The little wheels soon lost their shaped edges, and it was impossible to maintain the same cut for any length of time. Also the motor heated to such a point that I could hardly hold it.

Then, one day, during a discussion with a dentist friend about my frustration, he suggested that I might try diamond burs. Indeed, he even gave me a few that he felt were too worn or too rough to be used without possible injury to his patients. At last I found the perfect tool for me: the burs were long lasting and did not lose their shape. Next, I purchased, by mail order, a motor with a flexible shaft and a handpiece. The handpiece, when attached to the flexible shaft, holds the diamond bur. This whole assemblage avoids the unbearable heat of holding the motor in the hand. It is the type of equipment used by jewelers. At last, I was on my way, and my enthusiasm was even greater than before.

I certainly did not invent the use of diamond burs for glass engraving. But I had to discover it for myself, since I could find no written works on the subject. People who visit the art supply store that my wife and I own and who see the glass collection on display there are fascinated by it. They invariably ask where I learned to engrave glass, how it is done, and numerous people have asked if I would teach them the art. Lack of time and facilities prohibits my teaching, but I have endeavored in this book to pass along instructions and suggestions for those who would like to try glass engraving.

In the following chapters I will introduce you to the tools and equipment necessary to accomplish the desired results and will suggest which glass blanks to use and subjects to engrave. If you are an artist, or adept at drawing, so much the better. However, anyone who wants to can learn to use simple objects and designs to decorate glass. As with painting, you develop your own style as you progress. And, as with painting, you are limited only by your own imagination. Use my basic methods to get started, then experiment, innovate, and develop your own system. You will experience the thrill of exploring a new medium — glass — one of the earth's most plentiful resources.

INTRODUCTION

No one knows exactly when or where glass was first made. Legend has it that it was discovered by accident in a prehistoric campfire. The basic ingredients of glass are the simple compounds of silica, or sand, and potash, mixed and heated to a molten state, and these components for glass could have been there: sand and ash, with limestone pebbles to act as a flux, a substance used to promote the fusion of silica and potash. When these early people did discover glass, they made one of the most remarkable substances ever conceived by man. We do know that the art of glassworking is an ancient one. Beads and ornaments of fine quality by Egyptian and Phoenician artisans that date back three to four thousand years still exist today; these include the ones that appear as inlays in the Tutankhamen treasures. We also know that early Greeks and Romans prized certain types of glass more highly than precious metals and used glass chips profusely in their mosaic designs which were inlaid in the walls and walkways of their buildings.

However, the art of making the highly refined clear glass of the ancient Egyptian period was lost for centuries, finally surfacing again in Western Europe in about the twelfth century. From that time until about the thirteenth century, glassmaking and decorating led a rather roller-coaster existence due to civil disruptions, war, and squabbles among the glassmaking guilds of Central Europe. Many of the methods and techniques were lost during this period.

A revival of the ancient methods seems to have emerged in about the fourteenth century, with Venice at the center of the glassmaking art. Venetian craftsmen became highly skilled in forming, blowing, and coloring glass. It was also about this time that they began experimenting with diamond-point tools, with making scribed lines, and with stippling on glass (marking glass with a diamond or steel scriber, tapping dots and scribing lines to form the design). Later in the century, Germans began producing diamond-point engraved glass.

In the early sixteenth century, engraving with a copper wheel was introduced in Prague, Czechoslovakia, and glassmaking and decorating began to flourish in Holland, Germany, and England. In Belgium, Antwerp became the center for stipple engraving. Artisans there used a sliver of diamond placed in the end of a wooden holder to tap designs into the glass; the art of stipple engraving soon spread to England and the Scandinavian countries. Copperwheel engraving increased in popularity in all these countries, and artisans sometimes combined wheel engraving and diamond-point for unusual effects.

America's role in the glass industry began about 1608, when the first glassmaking house was established in Jamestown, Virginia. Henry William Stiegel, of the Flint Glass Manufactory, is credited with producing the first cut glass in America in 1771; today, Stiegel's pieces are highly prized by collectors. America introduced press-molded glass (a means of mechanically producing glass in great quantities) to the world in the early nineteenth century. Since that time, America has come to be a leader in the glass industry.

Of course, no treatise on American glass would be complete without mentioning Louis Tiffany. Tiffany was a pioneer in art glass — glass that is a work of art in addition to being utilitarian. His lamp shades and iridescent glass are still exhibited in museums throughout the world. Perhaps the ultimate in colorless glass today is produced by Steuben Glass of Corning Glass Works in New York. Steuben's purity and brilliance is unexcelled, and the engraved pieces are so prestigious that they are often presented as gifts to heads of state.

Glass — whether as vases, bowls, or objects of art — never loses its appeal. Add the dimension of engraving to its sparkling structure and behold — an irresistible work of art to rival any fine painting! Witness the beautiful stipple works that are part of the collection in the Victoria and Albert Museum of London. Study the superb glasswork and engraving created by Steuben and the Scandinavian firms of Orrefors and Kosta.

Brilliantly clear, bubble-free lead crystal glass is produced by glassmakers throughout the world. Lead crystal is basically made of silica and potash, with the addition of lead oxide and other components, probably known only to the individual glassmakers themselves. This glass is the ultimate working medium of the experienced engraver.

Glass, when hot, can be blown, drawn, shaped, molded, and colored. When cold, it can be cut, engraved, etched with acid, sandblasted, and stippled. This book pertains primarily to teaching the art of diamond bur engraving. However, it includes information about stipple and air abrasive (frosting areas on glass with an air eraser) techniques as well. Discussed are the tools required, and step-by-step instructions on how to use them to acquire the skill to complete finished engravings are provided. Any student with artistic talent, patience, dexterity, and practice can turn out a fine engraving worthy of displaying with justifiable pride.

1

GLASS ENGRAVING TECHNIQUES AND EQUIPMENT

In recent years, there has been a revival of interest in engraved glass on the part of collectors and practitioners alike. Unfortunately, there has been little information available on how it is accomplished for those who would like to try engraving. It is the purpose of this book to pass along to other artists the techniques that I use in the hope that they in turn can enjoy and help to perpetuate glass engraving. Too, it is the intention of this book to encourage an understanding and an appreciation for an ancient and beautiful art form.

TECHNIQUES
There are three methods used to engrave glass by cutting into the surface: copperwheel, stonewheel, and diamond bur. Although the first two are impractical for the amateur, an understanding of the principles involved is beneficial. These methods are described briefly to acquaint you with the tools and technique. However, diamond bur is the technique that will be used throughout this book.

Copperwheel Engraving
Copperwheel engraving is a highly skilled art and years of apprenticeship and experience are required to master the

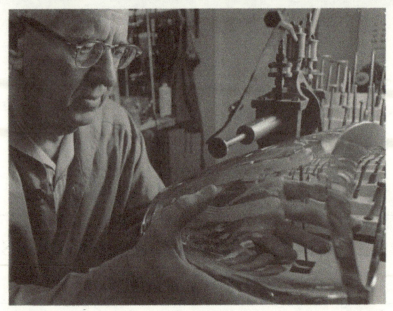

Copperwheel engraving. The glass is held in the hands and manipulated against the revolving copper wheel. Photograph by Con Keyes, courtesy of Reg Manning, Scottsdale, Arizona.

technique. The precision equipment, usually manufactured in Europe, is quite expensive. In this method, a copper wheel, chucked onto a steel shaft, is turned by a table-mounted lathe equipped with a variable speed control for the different cuts. The copper wheels are interchangeable and can vary in size from 1/16 inch (1.6 mm) to four or five inches (10.16 or 12.7 cm) in diameter. They are of various thicknesses and the cutting edges are square, rounded, or V shaped. A cutting abrasive, either silicon carbide or aluminum oxide in powdered form, is applied with a wedge-shaped felt strip that has been soaked in oil and attached so that it rides on the edge of the copper wheel. The revolving action of the wheel, along with the abrasive and oil mixture, makes the desired cut. The size of the wheel and the cut being made determine the revolving speed needed. The glass, or "metal," as it is called in the glass trade, is cradled in the hands and manipulated against the revolving copper wheel. The cuts made by copperwheel are smoother in texture than those made by diamond bur; otherwise, they are similar in appearance.

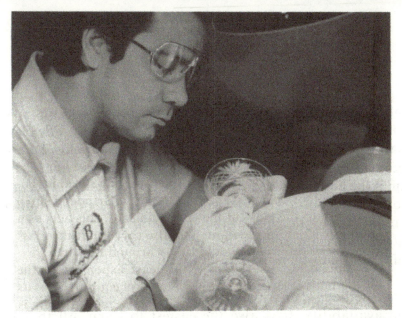

Michele Barone demonstrates stonewheel engraving. The glass is held by hand and brought into contact with the stone cutting wheel. Photograph courtesy of Barone Hand Cut Crystal.

Stonewheel Engraving

The stonewheel engraver uses manufactured abrasive stone wheels of a fine grit quality that range from the size of a shirt button to two feet (60.96 cm) or larger in diameter. These stones are attached to a table-mounted arbor (a spindle or axel for holding the cutting tools). The engraver can vary the speed, depending upon the size of the stone. The engraver shapes the stone edge for the required cut by wearing away part of the stone with a shaping tool. A wet sponge is held in place at the edge of the stone as a coolant; it also absorbs the glass and abrasive residue. The cuts are then polished, using a wood, lead, or cork wheel (usually mounted on a separate machine) and cerium oxide polishing powder. The beautiful "cut crystal" vases and bowls that you can purchase in many glass shops are made by stonewheel engraving methods.

Diamond Bur Engraving

Diamond bur engraving differs from the other two methods in that the cutting tool is held like a pencil in one hand with the glass being held in the other hand. This allows more flexibility than either the copperwheel or stonewheel process, since both the tool and glass can be maneuvered. A flexible shaft tool attached to a motor is used. At the opposite end of the shaft is a handpiece, which holds the diamond bur. The bur is the cutting instrument and the revolving speed is controlled by a foot-operated rheostat. Water is dripped from a container onto the glass at the spot being cut; this acts as a cutting lubricant and coolant, and also carries off the glass particles that otherwise would fly up around the cut.

Diamond bur engraving is the least expensive of the three methods of engraving glass because of equipment costs and availability. It is also the easiest to learn. All that is required are the tools, the desire to do it, and the determination to learn how.

Copperwheel, stonewheel, and diamond bur engravings are done on the outer surfaces of the vessel, not on the interior surface. The *intaglio* decoration (a design depressed below the surface of the material) of stonewheel engraving is usually meant to be viewed from directly in front of the surfaces on which it is executed. Copperwheel and diamond bur engravings, on the other hand, because they are to be viewed

The drawing at the left represents a profile in bas-relief as carved in stone. The drawing on the right shows that a glass engraving (depth exaggerated) cut intaglio, or into the surface, gives the same effect as the bas-relief when viewed from the opposite side of the engraving.

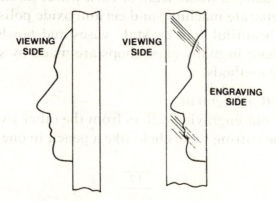

VIEWING SIDE   VIEWING SIDE

ENGRAVING SIDE

from the other side, are usually cut intaglio to give a *bas-relief* (raised) effect. (On occasion, the copperwheel or diamond bur engraver may wish to extend his design completely around the outside of a vase or bowl, and naturally, when this occurs, it would be quite impossible to view the entire design as a bas-relief.) The cuts made by copperwheel and diamond bur are usually not polished, but retain a "frosty" look caused by the cutting tool. However, the engraver does have the option to polish a portion of the engraving to emphasize or enhance a point.

EQUIPMENT

The following is the basic equipment required for diamond bur engraving:

One-tenth horsepower electric motor with flexible shaft
Detachable handpiece and three sizes of collets
Foot rheostat for motor speed control
About twelve different shapes and sizes of diamond-impregnated burs
Diamond pencil or carbide-tipped scriber
China marking pencil
Tracing paper
Carbon paper
Binocular-type magnifier that fits on the head
Mask or respirator
Good lighting
Water source
Convenient working area

The above is the minimum equipment needed to get started. You may wish to add more tools as you progress, and I will describe these in later chapters.

Because your source of supplies will vary, no exact cost figure can be given here; however, the beginner could expect to spend about $300 for the initial equipment. You will find a list of suppliers, who can furnish you with their equipment costs, and their addresses at the end of this book.

Motor

There are several brands and types of motors with attached flexible shafts available on the market; these are used in industry and in the jewelry trade. One type rests horizontally on a stand and sits on the working surface. The model I prefer hangs vertically from a stand. This offers more freedom of movement, takes less space, and allows plenty of elbow room in the working area. Such motors are available with one-tenth horsepower and can achieve up to 25,000 rpm when governed by a foot-operated speed control rheostat, which must be purchased separately. The flexible steel shaft is covered by a durable plastic composition sheath that allows great maneuverability.

The motor with attached flexible shaft has a price range of $50 to $90. If your budget allows, it is wise to purchase a good motor that will give long service and good performance. In using the motor, never apply so much pressure with the bur that the machine stalls; a sudden stoppage or overload could cause severe damage to the flexible shaft. The shaft should be lubricated after about fifty hours of use, and the motor about once every two hundred hours of use. Follow the manufacturer's instructions in caring for your motor to assure the best use of it.

Handpiece

The handpiece is the device that snaps into the flexible shaft of the motor and holds the diamond burs. It is held in the hand, somewhat like a pencil, when making the cut. The handpiece is made in various designs for specific purposes, but only the two that are best suited for glass engraving are described here. The first, shown here at the top of the photograph, has "no-oil" sealed bearings and a flexible spring connector. One collet (the part that fits into the chuck and clamps the diamond bur) is furnished with the handpiece; you can purchase separately the other two sizes needed. The three collets we will use are 1/16 inch (1.6 mm), 3/32 inch (2.3 mm), and 1/8 inch (3.17 mm); these are the sizes of the

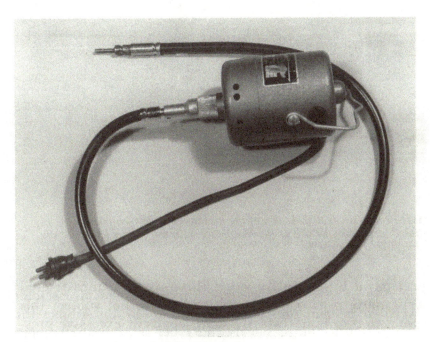

Electric motor with attached flexible shaft.

diamond bur shafts. The proper size collet is placed in the chuck, the diamond bur shaft is slipped into the collet, and, when the chuck is tightened, the tool is ready for use.

The handpiece shown at the bottom of the photograph has no chuck or collet; it does have a locking unit that holds the bur securely. It will only accept 3/32 inch (2.3 mm) shafts. Because of its configuration, this handpiece is especially handy for getting at small, hard-to-reach spots. Otherwise, it is structurally the same as the first.

The handpieces shown are equipped with a spring con-

Handpieces. The one shown at the top is the more versatile. The one at the bottom is used for small, hard-to-reach spots.

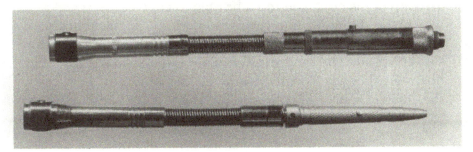

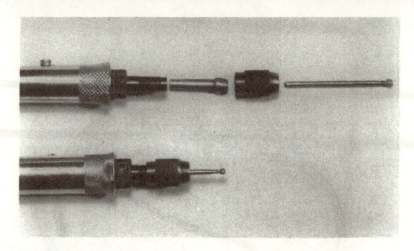

At the top is an exploded view of the handpiece, collet, chuck, and diamond bur. Below this is the handpiece with the bur secured into the chuck, ready for use.

nection of high-quality steel; this provides unrestricted wrist movement and great flexibility. Do not subject this connection to unnecessarily sharp bends or excessive pressure, as damage could result. The same handpieces are available without the spring connection, but I suggest using the former because of their versatility.

Take good care of your tools and they will serve you for a long time. At the close of each work session, remove the chuck and collet, dry with a rag or tissue, put a drop of oil on a rag, and wipe all parts to prevent rust. The second handpiece mentioned is more difficult to clean, but do it anyway! Shake out all water that has accumulated in the nozzle and dry with the corner of a folded rag inserted into the nozzle. Add a drop of oil and repeat the drying process. Always heed the manufacturer's instructions in caring for your equipment.

The Speed Control

To control the cuts, you must be able to control the speed at which the diamond bur revolves. Larger, rougher cuts require a fast speed, while delicate, smooth cuts require a slower speed. The device used to vary the speed is a foot-operated rheostat, located in the electrical circuit between the electric source and the motor. The greater the pressure

Rheostats. The foot-operated motor speed control device.

of your foot, the faster the motor will revolve. The rheostat provides smooth, precise control of motor speeds, and it automatically shuts off the motor when the foot is removed from the pedal. After some experience, you will be able to achieve the desired speed with ease; you will become unconscious of what your foot is doing — it will simply respond to your needs.

Of the two rheostat models shown on this page, I find the one with the dome-shaped top more versatile. You can press on the edge at any point for a reaction. Practice using the control when you begin your engraving exercises, especially the slow speed used in the finishing cut.

Do not expect the rheostat to last for the life of the motor. I have replaced the rheostat twice in the ten years or so that I have used my motor.

Diamond Bur

There are two types of diamond burs; they perform the same job, but differ in their construction. One is made of metal at the cutting point, with industrial-grade diamond dust, called bort, impregnated and metal-plated onto the surface. The other is a sintered type, formed with a bonding material that has the diamond throughout the cutting head, so that,

Diamond burs are available in many shapes and sizes. They are mounted on 1/16 inch (1.6 mm), 3/32 inch (2.3 mm), and 1/8 inch (3.17 mm) shafts.

as the diamond is worn away at the surface, there is more to replace it. Both types of diamond points are mounted on steel shafts in sizes of 1/16 inch (1.6 mm), 3/32 inch (2.3 mm), and 1/8 inch (3.17 mm), depending on the size of the cutting point.

Although the sintered type of bur costs a little more, it will last longer than the plated type. Once the diamond is gone on the plated type, there is nothing left but the steel core. I have a collection of both types in my workbox and use both to advantage. I usually use the plated burs for the rough cutting and the sintered burs for the more delicate work because the sintered burs seem to leave a smoother surface. It is not necessary, however, to use both types, since they are available in the same shapes and sizes. Diamond burs cost from about $5 to $18 each, depending on the size and type.

You will need the following diamond burs to begin your glass engraving ventures:

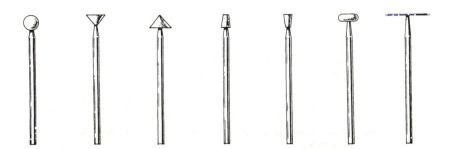

Diamond bur shapes. Left to right: *round, inverted cone, cone, tapered cylinder, inverted tapered cylinder, round-edge wheel, and saw.*

Three rounds in sizes 1 mm, 2 mm, and 4 mm
Two cone shapes in sizes 2 mm and 4 mm at the base
One inverted cone in size 3 or 4 mm
Round-edge wheels in sizes 6 and 10 mm
One tapered cylinder 3 mm at the base
One inverted tapered cylinder of the same size (3 mm)
One 3/4 inch (19 mm) flat saw
One 6 mm flat saw

The saw has diamond on the cutting edge only and is used to make thin line cuts and to help shape glass.

Of course, you will add other burs to your toolbox as you progress because there always seems to be a spot where the burs you have do not quite work. But finding the right bur is the challenge and fun of engraving. Dentist friends have given me slightly worn burs that they no longer can use on teeth. These often work beautifully on glass. It pays to visit your dentist!

Get to know the proper names of the burs, familiarize yourself with the task that each performs, and take care of them. I have some that I have used for several years and they will last several more.

Diamond Pencil
The diamond scriber or "pencil" is used to inscribe the design on the glass as a guide for the engraving. It is also used

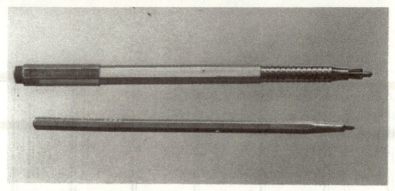

Scribers. Shown at the top is a typical diamond point scriber. Below it is a tungsten carbide scriber.

for engraving various tiny lines and for the stippling technique.

There are two types of diamond scribers. The first is made with a small sliver of uncut industrial-grade diamond set in either a wooden or plastic handle. Since the scriber has a rough, irregular-shaped diamond point, some edges of the diamond will cut small, sharp lines, while others will cut heavier or irregular lines. It is necessary to roll the scriber in your fingers while cutting on a piece of scrap glass to find a suitable cutting edge. Once this cutting point has been located, a mark can be placed on the holder for quick future reference.

The second type of scriber has a diamond that is precision ground to a point of either 60, 70, or 90 degrees and set in a plastic or aluminum holder. Some makers offer a model similar to a writing pen, complete with a clip and retractable point. The apex of the diamond cone in this type is always the cutting point, the advantage being that no matter which way the holder is turned, the point remains in a cutting position. This is the scriber I prefer. I use the one with a 90 degree angle point simply because, with the wider angle, it is the strongest and least likely to be damaged. Should your diamond become chipped or dulled, some manufacturers offer a sharpening service. A good diamond scriber can be purchased for under $10. Although diamond is the hardest substance known, it is brittle and can be chipped and damaged, so use it with a light touch.

Tungsten Carbide Steel Scriber

Used for the same purpose as and similar in appearance to a diamond scriber, the tungsten carbide-tipped scriber is less expensive. The cutting point is made of hardened tungsten carbide steel and is set in a holder of aluminum or plastic. The hard steel shaft protrudes about 3/16 inch (4.8 mm) from the holder. The shaft is about the size of a pencil lead and is shaped at a 30 degree angle to an exceedingly sharp point. Occasionally I use the carbide steel scriber with a straightedge to make long straight lines because the steel point glides smoothly against it without interruption. If the steel point becomes damaged and useless, the only choice is to buy a new one for two or three dollars.

Of the two scribers, I prefer the "feel" and sharp cutting ability of the diamond for freehand work, but you should try both scribers and judge the merit of each for your own preference.

Magnifier

You will need a binocular-type magnifier to protect your eyes and enable you to see clearly the scribed guidelines and details of the engraving. The water flowing over the surface tends to obscure details, so you need all the help you can get.

The binocular-type magnifier pictured here fits over the

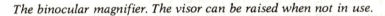

The binocular magnifier. The visor can be raised when not in use.

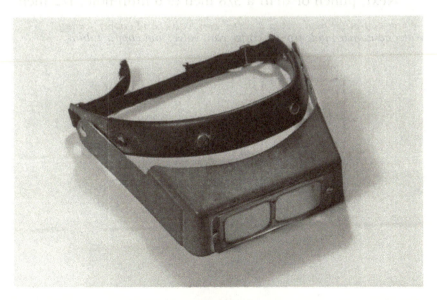

eyes with an adjustable headband and has a visor that flips up when not in use. I use one with a magnification of two and a half power, which allows about eight inches (20.32 cm) working distance from the subject; too much magnification does not allow you space enough between your nose and the glass to work.

In time, slurry (a mixture of water and ground glass) will spatter on the lenses, so it is necessary to clean them often. Use a wet tissue and wipe gently to avoid scratching the lens. Or allow tap water to flow over them for several minutes to dislodge the slurry and then wipe them gently with the tissue until dry and free of streaks.

Water Source

It is simple enough to rig up a gravity-feed water device by using easy-to-obtain materials. You will need a metal quart (946 ml) can (similar to a coffee can), a length of 1/4 inch (6.4 mm) copper tubing, and a shut-off valve for the tubing.

Get a twenty-four-inch (60.96 cm) length of tubing and a valve from an air conditioning or plumbing supply firm and have them make a 90 degree bend at the end, leaving about one inch (25.4 mm) straight after the bend. I suggest that you let the people where you buy the tubing bend the tube because it is almost impossible to keep it from collapsing if you are working without the proper tools.

Next, punch or drill a 3/8 inch (9.6 mm) hole, 1/2 inch

Water container made from a coffee can, valve, and copper tubing.

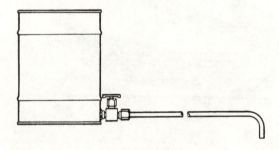

(12.8 mm) from the bottom of the can. Sand off all the painted surface of the can around the hole with number 180 grit sandpaper so it will accept solder. Insert the threaded end of the valve into the hole and solder it to the can. Punch or drill a 1/4 inch (6.4 mm) hole down about 1/4 inch (6.4 mm) from the top edge of the can on the opposite side from the valve. This hole serves as a place to attach a hanger for the can.

Wash the container inside and out with paint thinner, dry thoroughly, and give it a coat of primer and two coats of enamel paint to prevent rust and leakage. Slip the retaining nut off the valve onto the long, straight end of the tubing, insert the tubing into the valve, slide the nut down to the valve, and tighten it securely. You have your completed water device. If the tubing is too long for your work area, you can remove the tubing from the valve, cut it to the proper length with a hack saw, and place it back onto the valve.

Other types of water tanks may be used. Mine is a plastic container and tubing from a medical supply store. The container is of about one quart (946 ml) capacity, with a clear plastic tube attached to the bottom side. It hangs from a hook installed on the wall, about eighteen inches (45.7 cm) above the surface of the worktable. The plastic tubing, about twenty-four inches (60.96 cm) in length, is connected via a rubber section to a 1/4 inch (6.4 mm) copper tube that has a valve at the other end for regulating the water flow. The copper tube with the valve is attached to an expanding metal arm, which is placed on the wall above the work area; this is used to position the valve above the glass. The expanding arm was taken from an old wall lamp and is ideal for moving in and out and side to side above the work. The valve should be placed about twelve inches (30.48 cm) above the work surface, with the water container being about six inches (15.24 cm) above that.

A drip pan is used for catching the water and for a surface on which to place the glass while working. I use a rectangular aluminum cake pan filled with a two-inch (5.8 cm) layer of foam rubber. The foam rubber acts as a sponge to absorb the water and furnishes a safe place to rest the glass. The foam pad should be squeezed out frequently to dispose of the accumulated water drippings and the tiny glass particles that have settled in it. Although the glass particles are small, the glass dust could be irritating to your hands. The safest way to dispose of them is to take the pan with foam pad in it outside or to the sink, turn it up vertically, and brush off the surface with a stiff-bristle household brush. Rinse the pad and use gloves to wring out the remaining moisture.

Working Area

Your working area and the way you set it up is very important. You must be comfortable, with your equipment arranged conveniently. The motor should hang above and slightly behind your right shoulder (for left-handed people, the left shoulder), with the drip pan directly in front of you. A good light source should be above your head and to the

The ideal working area: good lighting, equipment located conveniently, and tools within easy reach.

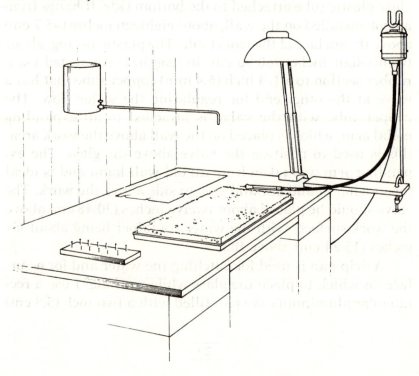

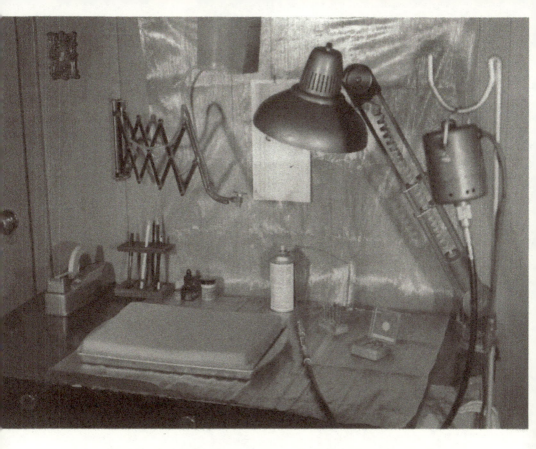

My work area. Notice the expanding arm device for the water spigot.

side of the arm you are using to hold the handpiece. Arrange your chair so that the desk or work surface is about midchest high. Remember, you are doing close work, using head binocular magnifiers, so you will want to be comfortable and not stoop over your work. The motor speed control should be right at your foot and the diamond burs and collets should be within easy reach on top of the workbench.

I use an ordinary home-office desk, with an extra-large top, placed against the wall of my studio as a workbench. The wall and desk top are covered with a plastic drop cloth to protect them from the spattering glass slurry. The drawers of the desk act as storage space for my ever-growing supply of tools. A one-inch by four-inch (25.4 mm by 10.16 cm) pine board is clamped on the right front edge of the desk

Motor rack made from a 3/8 inch (9.5 mm) steel rod and C clamps.

and extends out about ten inches (25.4 cm); this serves as a mount for the motor. I had a machine shop make the motor hanger to my design. It is constructed with a 3/8 inch (9.5 mm) steel rod welded to the back of a C clamp, with the top of the rod bent into a U shape on which the motor hangs. The clamps on the board and desk were used instead of screws because this allows easy removal of the unit for cleanup. The speed control is placed on the floor, usually under the desk, within easy reach of my foot.

You can also easily make a bur and collet holder to place on top of your workbench so that they will be within easy reach while you are working. Buy a one-inch (25.4 mm) by four-inch (10.16 cm) by six-inch (15.24 cm) piece of white pine from the lumber yard. Mark a line one inch (25.4 mm) from the edge of both sides on the upper surface along the length of the board. Then starting 3/4 inch (19.0 mm) from the end, drill six 1/8 inch (3.2 mm) holes to a depth of 3/8 inch (9.5 mm) at 3/4 inch (19.0 mm) intervals on both lines. These holes are for holding the burs. Measure another 3/4 inch (19.0 mm) from the last holes and drill two 1/4 inch (6.4 mm) holes to the depth of 3/8 inch (9.5 mm) on both lines and one hole of the same size and depth centered between these; the three holes are for the collets. Sand the block of wood and apply two coats of marine varnish. You can make the block as long as you wish and drill more holes, but I seldom use more than six or eight types of burs at a sitting and leave the ones I am not using in my toolbox.

Good lighting is a necessity! In addition to a ceiling light in my studio, I have an adjustable incandescent fluorescent combination lamp clamped to the edge of the desk. It moves up or down, backward or forward, and has a ball joint that allows me to tilt the shade to avoid direct light from the lamp to the eyes. Different pieces of glass sometimes require different positions of the lamp in order to prevent reflected glare.

Completing my work area is the water container and adjustable arm that I described previously.

This is my work set-up. Much of it is improvised, but is convenient and adequate for my needs. You may have a different situation, but can design your own work area to fit the available space by using my diagrams as a guide.

Bur and collet holder made from a block of white pine.

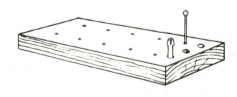

2

GETTING STARTED

You may feel a bit apprehensive when you confront your first piece of glass. Do not despair. You have a powerful tool right at your fingertips—diamond! Glass is hard, but diamond is many times harder and it cuts glass with ease. As you experience your first practice cuts, you will have a growing sense of confidence that you really can create something beautiful from that plain piece of glass.

Now that you are acquainted with your tools and the working area is set up, it is time to get started learning the basic cuts. Practice until you master the exercises outlined here because they are the procedures you will use in doing all of your glass engraving. *Important warning:* Do not attempt to cut the glass dry. Your expensive diamond burs will be ruined if used without water as a coolant and lubricant. The glass dust is harmful because long term inhalation of silica from glass can cause silicosis, or fibrosis of the lungs.

THE FIRST CUT
Purchase several pieces of 1/4 inch (6.4 mm) plate glass about four inches (10.16 cm) square. Have the edges and corners ground smooth to prevent cuts on your hands as you hold the glass during the engraving process.

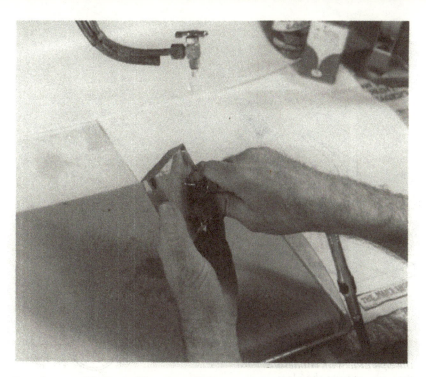

Practice cut. The round bur is pulled toward the operator.

Select the 2.3 mm-size collet for the 4 mm round diamond bur and chuck it securely into the handpiece with thumb and forefinger; never use pliers to do this. There is a hole at the base of the chuck into which you can insert a nail to keep the chuck from turning as you tighten it.

Open the water valve to the point where you get a drop of water about every second. With the glass in your left hand, handpiece in your right (the other way around if you are left handed), activate the motor with your foot on the rheostat to about half speed and touch the bur, held at an angle similar to the one used when writing with a pencil, to the glass at the point where the water falls on it. *Never cut dry!* That can ruin the bur, the glass, and send fine glass particles into the air around you. Very dangerous!

Now, pull the diamond tool toward you with moderate pressure of the bur against the glass. Using too much pressure will force the cut; let the diamond do the cutting. You will soon learn when the pressure is just right. Make the cut about one inch (25.4 mm) long, then repeat the action on the

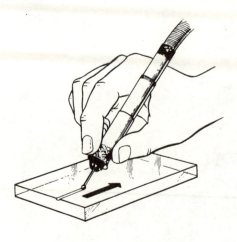

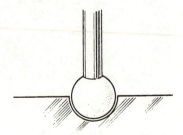

Above: *The bur is pulled toward the operator with moderate pressure against the glass.*

Right: *The cut is made to a depth of about one-half the diameter of the round bur.*

same area until the depth of the cut is half the diameter of the round bur. Turn the glass over and look at it from the other side. The finished piece will be viewed from the opposite side of the cut, so get into the habit of checking your progress often from that side.

You will notice that there are small chips or ragged breaks along the edges of the cut. The next step is the smoothing or finishing cut. Cut the water supply down to about half the amount you used on the original cut. Press the foot control very gently so that you can obtain a speed that is as slow as you can maintain without stalling. Introduce the bur to the edge of the cut using a very light touch. Pull the tool toward you, but this time hold the bur and handpiece at an angle that is about 45 degrees from the plane of the cut. As you pull the tool toward you, exert a very slight pressure of the bur on the side of the cut nearest you. Repeat

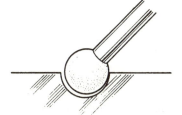

Above: *The smoothing cut. Use a slow speed and pull at an angle against the sides of the cut.*

Right: *To smooth the edge of the cut, the bur is pulled along the side of the cut, using a slow motor speed.*

this stroke until the chipped edge is cut away. Turn the glass around so that the other rough edge is nearest you and repeat the operation to smooth that edge. When you are satisfied with the edges, check your work from the opposite side of the glass. Looks pretty good, doesn't it?

As time goes by, you will notice (if you have not already) that the bur will sometimes get out of control; the torque and traction of the revolving bur can pull it over the side of the cut and make an unwanted mark on the glass. These accidents do happen, especially during the learning process, but occasionally even an old hand has one of these exasperating experiences. You can't erase the mark, but you can in some cases change the design to cover the mishap. If an accident such as this does occur, don't despair; with practice you can learn to control the action so that this seldom happens.

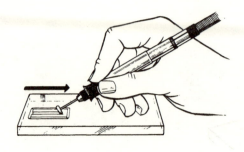

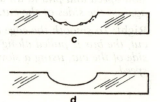
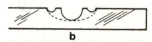
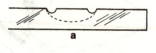

Above: *Cutting out a large area.*
Right: *Steps in cutting out a large area.*
Cross section view: (a) *cut outline with a*
round bur; (b) *cut out center with a*
round-edge wheel; (c) *intermediate cuts*
with round-edge wheel; and (d) *smooth the*
cut with a round bur.

THE BIG CUT

Some engravings, such as a tree trunk, or the torso of an animal, bird, or human, will have large cut areas. In this exercise, we will use the same 4 mm round bur to make a rectangular cut about 3/4 of an inch (19 mm) wide by 1 1/2 inches (3.81 cm) long. Deviating from your previous free-hand practice strokes, begin by marking the outline of the rectangle with a china marking pencil. Then, using the diamond pencil, scribe a light line about 1/32 inch (.77 mm) inside your pencil line. Always scribe your pattern a fraction smaller than the planned design. Employing the same principle as the previous cut and using the same amount of water, proceed to overcut the scribed line in order to cut out any tiny breaks caused by the diamond pencil on the surface. Always overcut in this manner for engravings where you are using a scribed line. Now following the guidelines, cut the outline of the rectangle with the bur as you did in the previous cut, but this time the cut should be only about half as deep.

Carefully smooth the outer edges of the rectangle as before to remove the rough spots and chips. Next, change to the 10 mm round-edge wheel and open the water valve to allow more water to drip on the glass. As you did when using the smaller round bur, draw the cutting tool toward you down the center (lengthwise) of the rectangle, from end to end. Repeat the cut until you have a concave surface about 1/8 inch (3.17 mm) deep from one end to the other. Now join this center cut to the edge of the rectangle outline cut. To do this, use the 10 mm round-edge wheel in the same manner as above and cut at the edge and on both sides of the big center cut until you have reached the edge of the outline cut. In effect, you are making a concave, partially cylindrical cut, 1 1/2 inches (38.1 mm) long by 3/4 inch (19 mm) wide by 1/8 inch (3.17 mm) deep. At this time the cut should be roughly to shape; however, you will have to make intermediate cuts to smooth out the contour by overlapping the cuts already made.

THE FINISHING OR SMOOTHING CUT

A rough surface that should be smooth or a ragged edge on a cut can spoil an otherwise beautiful engraving. Practice perfecting the smoothing cut in order to avoid this unappealing condition. Remember, the slower the speed of the revolving bur, the smoother the cut. This holds true with any shape bur you use.

You can use a round bur and the 4 mm round-edge wheel for smoothing. A barrel-shaped sintered bur, 10 mm in diameter, is my favorite for putting the finishing touch on the larger cuts. The idea behind this cut is not only to

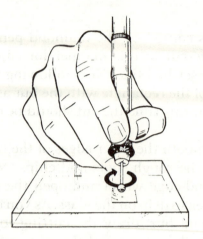

Smoothing a large area. Use a circular motion with a light touch.

smooth out the bumps but also to put a finer finish on the surface of the cut. I like to use a sintered bur or a well-worn round one. As the burs are used, some of the surface diamond tends to wear off, so they do not cut as quickly; but they make ideal smoothing tools.

For this exercise, put a smooth finish on the concave surface of the rectangle by using the 10 mm round-edge wheel in the handpiece. Use very little water for this procedure — only enough to allow a white glass residue to build up around the bur as you cut. Keeping the water to a minimum allows the abrasive action of the residue to help smooth the cuts, and you will be able to see the work better without the reflective influence of the water. Use a slow speed and a very light touch. Cut in a circular motion, back and forth, up and down. Do not work too long in any one place; go over the entire surface repeatedly.

Wash off the residue that has accumulated and, while it is still wet, look at the surface by tilting the glass to and fro, side to side. You will be able to spot the highlights which indicate high points. Mark these high spots with a graphite pencil, which will not be affected by the water flow, and proceed to cut them down with the same gentle cutting motion. Wash the glass again and repeat the procedure until the surface is smooth. Turn the glass over and look at the work from the front (viewing) side. Always check your work from the viewing side, and if you detect uneven spots, mark them with the graphite pencil on the cut surface while still viewing from the front side. Now turn your work over again to work out the marked blemishes.

I cannot overemphasize the importance of a smooth finish, so practice this procedure until you have perfected it.

OTHER TECHNIQUES

Flat Saw. I use a flat saw attached to the handpiece to cut thin lines representing grass stems, small tree branches, or any design where a long thin line is needed. Use the saw in the manner shown in the illustration on this page. Because the saw cuts very quickly, I use my thumb against the glass as a kind of depth regulator to keep the saw from going too deep. Use a slow speed, but more water than in the smoothing cut.

Practice making parallel cuts about 1/8 inch (3.17 mm) apart and an inch (25.4 mm) or so long. Do not mark guidelines for this exercise—do them freehand. Try to keep the lines straight and parallel, and cut only as deep as the blade is thick. After eight or ten lines, turn the glass and cut several perpendicular lines across the first lines, maintaining the same depth. For the last few lines, increase the speed of the saw. Inspect the crosshatched lines from both the front and the back of the glass. Notice that the slower speed pro-

Using the saw to cut a long, straight line.

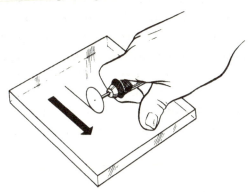

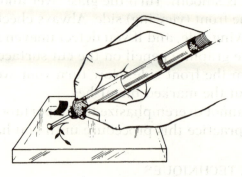

Using the inverted cone to cut leaves.

duces smoother lines, especially at the points where the lines intersect.

Inverted Tapered Cylinder and Inverted Cone. These are used in the same manner as the flat saw when cutting a straight line with a sharp angular cut. I also use the inverted cylinder for texturing; you can make tree bark by pulling the bur toward you at a 45 degree angle and making short cuts. Use the inverted cone at a high angle for cutting leaves; a short dipping cut with the inverted cone, bringing the bur sharply up at the end of the stroke, forms a perfectly clean end on the leaf. The cone shape is useful in making sharp, narrow corners as well as cone-shaped cuts. Experiment with all the other bur shapes and sizes that I have recommended to determine for yourself which bur will do which job for you.

Frosting. Another useful technique you will want to practice is frosting, so called because it gives the appearance of frost on a window pane. Frosting can be used effectively to simulate fleecy clouds or mist or whitecaps on distant water. It can be used to fill in the surface between the scribed lines of an initial or any design that needs a shallow, matte background. The 2 mm and 4 mm round burs are used for frosting. For the following exercise, I suggest starting with the 4 mm bur. Use just enough water to keep the glass wet,

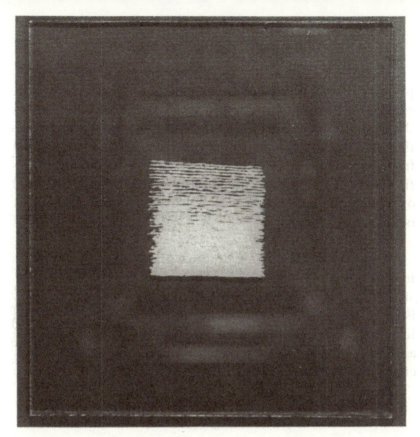

"Frosting." Use a light touch with a round diamond bur.

activate the motor to a slow speed, and barely touch the revolving bur to the glass. As you move the bur in a straight line across the glass, notice that it makes a narrow, skipping line. Immediately beside this line make another one, just touching the first line, then another and another, until you have a strip about 1/2 inch (12.7 mm) wide. Examine the results: note the small, irregular spaces where the lightly held bur did not touch the glass, giving the overall area a sparkling appearance.

Next, repeat the same procedure on a new area of the glass, but this time leave about the width of the line between each of the lines. Now repeat the second exercise in an area of about the same size as the first one, then crosshatch the lines at about a 90 degree angle for a different look. For the next exercise, scribe a one inch (25.4 mm) square on your practice glass with a diamond pencil. Start on one side of the square and frost it completely solid, but gradually lighten the pressure as you go to the opposite side of the square so that it is faintly filled in and you have an area graduated from light to dark. Finally, frost another area on your practice glass by using a circular motion with the bur, over and over until the area is completely frosted; the swirling effect is quite distinctive.

Fill every inch of your practice glass, using all the tools to find out what each will do. Make deep cuts, shallow cuts, straight and curved cuts. You are not trying to make a finished piece at this time, just getting to know the tools and learning to control them. Turn the glass to the viewing side and notice the cut shapes and the interesting textures. Glass engraving is fascinating, even at this stage!

3

Engraving Forms: Projects

After you have gotten the feel of the handpiece and how the various burs, wheels, and saws perform, it is time to engrave a form. You will be working in reverse so that objects that come forward on the viewing side as bas-relief are actually cut deeper into the engraving. To better illustrate this point, hold a piece of flat glass in front of you with your left hand. Place your right forefinger against the glass on the opposite side. Imagine that your right finger is a drill bit and you are drilling a hole into the glass toward your face. The resulting imaginary hole would appear to be coming out toward you. After time and practice you will get oriented to this reverse sculpting.

TREE

I chose a tree for the first subject because it is relatively uncomplicated and therefore among the easier forms to engrave. You don't have to stay within exacting confines to do this tree or follow a set pattern. Besides, if your bur should get out of control and slip over the edge, you can always add another limb to cover the mistake. Trees are my favorite subject. I have done many of them and there is always some-

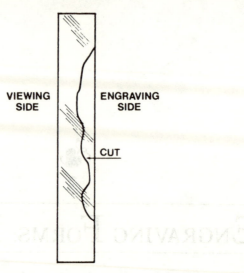

VIEWING SIDE

ENGRAVING SIDE

CUT

When the cut is made intaglio, or into the surface of the glass, it appears to come forward in bas-relief when viewed from the opposite side of the glass.

thing exciting in shaping the trunk, texturing the bark, and adding the limbs and branches.

Don't aim for a specific type of tree this time — just a composite one. As you become more proficient you will want to try both coniferous and deciduous trees. Pines are interesting, and they fit on a tall narrow vase or glass beautifully. Oaks are a challenge, and with the bending, twisting branches, it is possible to attain great depth and dimension. I like to do old gnarled trees with deep bark and lots of knots and broken limbs. Occasionally, I will engrave a stylized tree and use the inverted cone bur to cut each individual leaf. I would venture to say that sooner or later trees will become your favorite subject too.

For this first finished engraving, you should again use a piece of the inexpensive plate glass that you used for all your practice. The glass should be four inches square (10.16 cm) and 1/4 inch (6.4 mm) thick. Draw the design directly on the glass with a china marking pencil. Draw the trunk and main limbs first, leaving out the small branches and twigs. These will be added after the bulk of the tree has been established. Use the diamond pencil to scribe the outline of the tree, being careful to scribe just inside the china pencil mark. The

The outline of the tree is drawn on glass with a china marking pencil.

pencil mark is then washed off, leaving the scribed lines as a guide. There is no point in putting detail inside the scribed drawing, because it would only be cut away. This is the reason I usually make a detailed drawing and hang it on the wall in front of me to use as a guide while I work. However, do not use a drawing for this engraving; allow yourself more freedom to interpret the subject your own way.

Following the pencil lines, the outline of the tree is scribed on the glass with the diamond pencil.

Put the 4 mm round bur in the collet of the handpiece and adjust the water flow to about one drop per second. The trunk is outlined with the round bur, just cutting out the scribed guidelines. Next, the main limbs are cut, using the 6 mm round-edge bur. Now go back to the 4 mm bur to cut the tapering limbs and add the smaller limbs. Before putting in the branches and twigs, chuck the 10 mm round-edge wheel and start cutting out the bulk of the trunk. You get a much better perspective of the subject by working the overall mass, rather than developing a small area to its finish; painters do this in order to balance color values and space. Although you are not working with color or on a one-dimensional plane, you do need to be always conscious of the mass of the pattern that you are executing. Turn the glass over to the viewing side to check your progress often. Are you still with me? How does your tree look at this time?

Continue on the engraving side of the glass until the entire bulk of the trunk and main limbs are cut in and there are nice rounded forms on both. The smaller branches are cut next, using the 2 mm round bur. Then the smallest branches are cut with the 1 mm round bur. Use the 2 mm to smooth the edges of the trunk and all the limbs.

Now add a sawn-off limb to the front side of the trunk. If you have objects that come forward from the main body of the engraving and other objects that recede to the background, you add dimension and interest to a piece. Always keep in mind that you are sculpting intaglio, so that when the object is viewed from the other side of the glass it appears as bas-relief sculpture. Use the 6 mm round-edge wheel to cut the limb. Start at the top of the limb and cut deeper, allowing the flat top of the bur to form the sawn-off part of the limb. The cut is gradually shallowed to its base at the trunk. This is not done with one cut, but requires repeated work until the proper depth is reached.

After you are satisfied that the protruding limb is well formed, continue to give it more character by adding the

The trunk and limbs are cut, using a 10 mm and a 4 mm round bur.

The trunk and limbs are smoothed and the smaller branches are cut with the 1 mm round bur.

The tree is cut about 2 mm in depth. Note the depth of the protruding broken limb.

After the branches and twigs are added, the bark texturing finishes the engraving.

bark texture. Using the 3 mm inverted tapered cylinder bur, make short, irregular cuts over the entire trunk and main limbs, letting them diminish toward the ends of the limbs. Turn the glass to the viewing side and check your progress on the bark. Finish texturing the smaller limbs with the 1 mm round bur. The smallest branches are added with the same round bur and finally the twigs are cut in with the 6 mm flat saw.

Wash the piece of glass with clean water, dry, and check it from the viewing side. Make any needed corrections, then sign your name and put the date on it with the diamond pencil on the viewing side, so it can be read as the viewer looks at the glass. Congratulations! You have just completed your first glass engraving.

GEOMETRIC DESIGN

Geometric designs are exciting to work, especially on prisms or any glass object that is multi-sided so that it reflects the engraving and repeats itself in the other sides or planes of the glass. Even on the flat practice glass that is used in this exercise, geometric designs can be very interesting. You can use circles, squares, triangles, or any other geometric figure, singly or in a combination, to create a work of art. These forms are a challenge to engrave because of the necessity of having to maintain straight lines, gentle arcs, and angles. This is very good practice for the student at this stage of the learning process.

The design for this exercise includes the triangle, rhombus (diamond shape), and the circle. These geometric forms are used here to create an aquarium motif. The rhombus becomes the fish's body, the triangle becomes the caudals or tail fins, and the circles represent the bubbles.

Use the same type and size practice glass as before: four inches (10.16 cm) square and 1/4 inch (6.4 mm) thick. Use the design as a guide. With a china marking pencil and a ruler, draw the diamond shapes that represent the fishes'

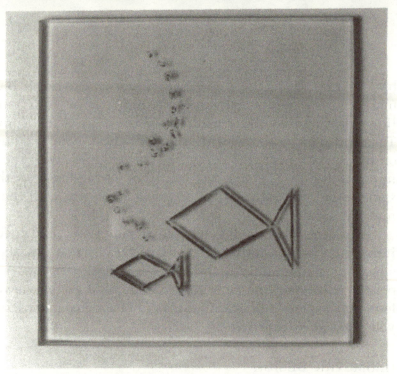

A china marking pencil and ruler are used to draw the design on the glass.
(Engraving side)

The design is scribed on the glass with the diamond pencil, and the pencil
lines are washed off. (Engraving side)

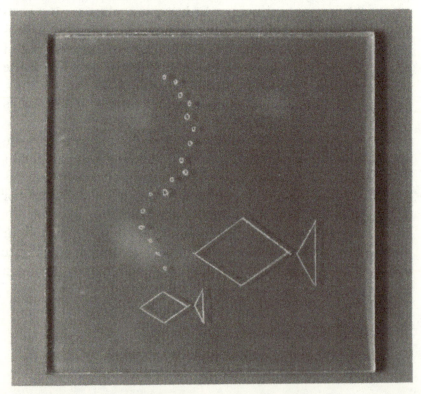

bodies and add the triangle shapes to indicate the tails. Mark the position of the air bubbles with a dot or small circle. Do not mark the crosshatching on the sides of the fish; these lines will be cut later without using a guide. Now with the diamond pencil, and using the ruler as a straightedge, scribe just inside the penciled lines of the figures. Scribe the air bubbles with a small circle or a dot.

The engraving phase of the project is the next step. Wash the pencil marks off the glass so you have an unobstructed view of the scribed lines as a guide for cutting. Chuck the 2 mm round diamond bur into the handpiece and adjust the water flow to about one drop per second. Start at any corner of the larger rhombus, and make a light cut exactly on the scribed line to the next corner, using a medium motor speed. Be sure that your first cut is steady and straight. Repeat the cut over and over until the depth is about one third the diameter of the 2 mm bur. Continue cutting the remaining outlines of the diamond shapes in the same manner, main-

The outline cuts are made, starting with the larger fish design. (Engraving side)

The smaller fish is outlined, the crosshatch cuts are made on the larger fish, and some of the air bubbles are cut. (Engraving side)

taining straight lines and a constant depth. Cut the triangle of the larger figure in the same way, using the same 2 mm round bur. After all lines of the larger fish are cut, start smoothing these cuts. Use a slow motor speed, less water, and a light touch to smooth both sides of the cuts with the 2 mm round bur. Cut and smooth the lines of the smaller fish in the same manner. Wash the glass, dry it, and inspect the cuts for irregularities and correct them.

Cut the smaller air bubbles with the 2 mm round bur, using a slow to medium motor speed, with the water flowing a drop per second. Use the handpiece and bur as if it were a drill, holding the bur in one spot, exactly on the scribed mark. This action creates a round indentation in the glass surface and, when viewed from the other side, gives the impression of a sphere. Use light pressure at the finish of the cut for smoothing. Vary the sizes of the smaller air bubbles by drilling deeper or shallower cuts. Use the 4 mm round diamond bur for the larger bubbles.

Finally, the crosshatch lines are cut inside the diamond shapes to simulate the scales of the fish; the 3/4 inch (19 mm) flat saw is used for this purpose. Again, the water flow is about a drop per second and the motor speed is slow. Hold the handpiece so that the saw is perpendicular to the surface of the glass and make four or five parallel cuts very closely together (about 1 mm apart) diagonally across the side of the fish. Then make four or five cuts diagonally across the first cuts to give a crosshatch effect. The slower these cuts are made, the smoother they will be. The depth should be only a fraction of 1 mm.

Wash the glass, dry it, and make any needed corrections. Sign your name on the viewing side of the glass to finish your creation. You now have a simple, yet attractive, work of art.

Remember to clean, dry, and oil the chuck of the handpiece after every session of using it.

The finished engraving from the viewing side of the glass.

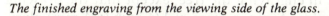

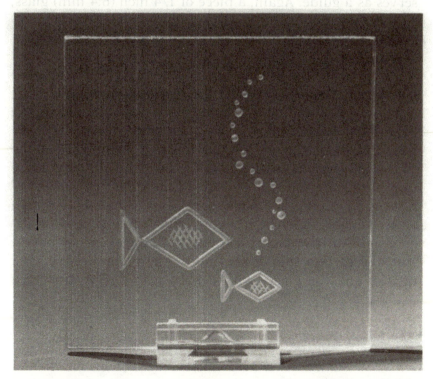

Drawing of a horse head design (side two, or engraving side of the drawing). *Use this design as a guide and draw it on tracing paper. The overall drawing should be 2 1/2 inches (63.6 mm) tall.*

HORSE HEAD

In this exercise, you will go a step further and make a detailed drawing of a more complex subject on paper before the engraving begins. The procedure is basically the same as the one used in engraving the tree, except that the drawing serves as a guide. Again, a piece of 1/4 inch (6.4 mm) glass, four inches square (10.16 cm) is used for this engraving. Follow the drawing of the horse head shown above for your engraving.

I drew a stylized horse head for this assignment because it is simpler to engrave than a realistic one. Make your drawing on parchment tracing paper and then flip the parchment over and retrace the lines on the back side of the paper. This is necessary in order to check the progress of the engraving from both the viewing side and the engraving side. Designate the viewing side of the drawing "side one" and the engraving side "side two." Now, using masking tape on two edges, tape the drawing with side one against the glass and side two facing you. Slide a piece of carbon paper, with the carbon side down toward the glass, between the tracing and the glass. With a hard lead pencil, trace the

The drawing is taped to the glass and carbon paper is used between the drawing and glass to transfer the image to the glass. (Engraving side)

Scribed lines on the glass, just inside the carbon outline. (Engraving side)

drawing to transfer the horse head onto the glass. Remove the tracing and keep it to use as a reference while you are engraving.

You now have a faint drawing of the horse head on the glass. Use the diamond pencil or steel scriber to scribe the outline of the head on the glass. Draw the scribed lines just inside the transferred carbon lines. You now have a permanent outline of the horse head scribed on the glass as a guide for the engraving.

Chuck the 4 mm round diamond bur into the handpiece, adjust the water flow to about one drop per second, and proceed to cut the outline of the head with this bur, right on the scribed outline. Use a medium speed and let the diamond do the cutting; don't push or force the cut. Continue cutting until the line is about 1/8 inch (3.2 mm) wide and about 1/16 inch (1.6 mm) deep. Do not try to cut the line to this width and depth in one pass of the diamond bur. Instead, gradually work it to the proper size using several passes; this assures a smoother, cleaner cut. You will need to switch to the smaller 2 mm round bur to cut the points of the ears. Smooth the outline cut with the same round burs using a slow speed and less water. Wash and dry the glass, turn it to the viewing side and inspect the outline cut for irregular or rough spots. Correct these places, as instructed in the practice session. You are now ready to cut out the inside bulk of the head and neck.

Use the round-edge wheel as you did for the "Big Cut" (page 38) in the practice session and make a cut in the center of the head and neck to a depth of about 1/8 inch (3.2 mm). Now, with the 4 mm round bur, start cutting in from the outline toward the center, gradually getting deeper until you reach the depth of the center cut. Continue this procedure to cut out the bulk of the head and neck. You will now have a concave engraving of the horse head without any detail feature. Use the 4 mm round bur, with a slow speed and less water, to smooth the entire head design. Remember to check the engraving for high spots; mark and smooth them

The first cut with the diamond bur outlines the design. Cut on the scribed line. (Viewing side)

This cut, in the center of the head and neck, establishes the depth of the engraving. (Viewing side)

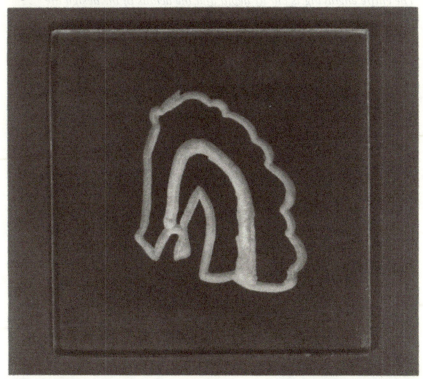

as previously instructed. Wash the glass, dry it, and check your progress from the viewing side. After you are satisfied that the engraving is clean and smooth, use side two of the original drawing as a guide and pencil in the details — eye, ear, nostril, face bones, and mane — of the horse head on the engraved design (the pencil lead will not be erased by the flow of water on the frosted surface). The frosted surface of the glass takes pencil beautifully.

There is no set sequence to cutting the details. You can begin at any point and work back and forth from one area to another. However, for this lesson begin at the nose and work it to completion, and then go on to the other details.

Use the 1 mm round bur and, again, adjust the water flow to about one drop per second. Using the penciled guideline, cut deep around the nostril to form the nostril lobe. Leave the nostril opening (in the center of the lobe) shallow, because it is an opening that goes deep within the nose. Since we are engraving intaglio, or into the surface, the nostril opening should appear deeper than the nose surface when viewed from the other side of the glass. Turn the glass

The entire engraving is cut to depth and the details of the design are drawn on the frosted glass with pencil. (Viewing side)

to the viewing side to check your work and also to check it with side one of your original drawing. When you are satisfied that the nostril lobe is both deep and smooth enough, start tapering out this cut to the depth of the nose surface so that you attain a smooth transition from the nostril to the nose.

Next, cut the lips and teeth with the 1 mm round bur, using a slow speed. Now, using the 2 mm round bur, cut the line that indicates the nose bone from the nostril to the cheek bone near the eye. When this appears to look right to you and is smooth, cut in the eyeball with the same 2 mm round bur; this will be just a concave oval. Then, change to the 2 mm inverted cone bur, holding it at a high angle, and, using just the sharp edge of the bur, cut the eyelids around the eye; this cut requires a slower speed. Check your work from the viewing side (number one) with the original drawing. The ear is next; use the 2 mm round bur to get a smooth, concave surface. Finish the point of the ear with the 1 mm round bur. At this point, wash the glass, dry it, and compare the engraving with both sides of the drawing. Get into the habit of doing this often — it may save you many problems later in the engraving.

The next step is to cut the semicircle that indicates the jaw bone. With water flow the same (one drop per second), use the 4 mm round bur for this. Cut in deeply because the jaw bone is a prominent feature of the head design. Taper this cut inside the semicircle so that it gradually becomes level with the surface of the face. Smooth the jaw and nose areas. Cut the line that indicates the neck muscle, which extends from the jaw, down the neck, and on to the bottom of the design. Use the 4 mm round bur and cut in deep, since this, too, is a prominent feature in the design. Make a smooth, rounded taper up from the depth of this cut to the surface of the surrounding neck area. Smooth the area and check your work from the viewing side.

The last step is to cut the mane of the horse's head. This is an interesting area that strongly influences the overall de-

The finished engraving. (Viewing side)

sign. Keep the water flow the same as above. Use the round burs to cut the mane: the 4 mm one for the large areas, tapering to the smaller areas with the 2 mm and the 1 mm round burs. Smooth these cuts carefully and check them from the viewing side, comparing your engraving with the original drawing (side one). If the engraving is to your satisfaction, sign your name and date the piece on the viewing side of the glass, opposite your engraving. Your third project is finished.

FLOWER

I chose a universal favorite—the daisy—for your next engraving assignment. Floral designs are not only appealing to almost everyone, they are also interesting subjects to engrave. The petals and leaves are cut rather shallow, because to cut them deep would destroy the delicate look of the plant. Use the drawing shown here as a guide. Place a piece of tracing paper over it and pencil in the daisy. Mark this "side two"—the engraving side of the drawing. Remove the tracing, turn it over, and pencil the daisy on the other side of the paper following the same lines — "side one," or the viewing side cf the drawing.

Use a practice glass that is 1/4 inch (6.4 mm) by 4 inches (10.16 cm) square. Tape the tracing of the daisy, with side two out toward you, onto the glass with masking tape. Slide a piece of carbon paper, carbon side down, between the tracing and the glass. Then, using a hard lead pencil, trace the drawing of the flower to transfer the image to the glass. Remove the tape and drawing from the glass and place the drawing within easy reach. You will need it while you are engraving to use as a reference to check your progress. Checking your work often, from both the engraving side (side two of the drawing) and the viewing side (side one of the drawing) is essential. Do not hurry the work! If you find yourself tired or impatient, stop and rest awhile before resuming work. I used about eight working hours engraving the daisy design shown here.

After you have removed the drawing from the glass, use the diamond pencil or steel scriber to scribe the design on the glass. Scribe just a little way inside the carbon lines of your design. You are now ready for the first cut with the diamond bur. The daisy engraving requires the use of four

Trace this drawing, using tracing paper, as a guide for engraving the flower design.

The carbon paper is placed between the glass and drawing and held in place with masking tape. (Engraving side)

diamond burs: the 1 mm round, the 2 mm round, the 4 mm round, and the 3/4 inch (19 mm) flat saw.

The first cut will be the outline cut, using the 2 mm round bur. Adjust the water flow to about a drop of water per second and use a medium motor speed (about midway between the slowest and fastest speed of your motor). Proceed to cut on the scribed lines of the entire design. Cut to a depth of about one third the diameter of the 2 mm round bur. Do not try to cut to this depth in one pass: gradually work to the proper depth. Outline the petals and leaf in this manner. Wash the glass and dry it with a soft paper towel or cloth. Inspect your work and compare it to the drawing from both the engraving and viewing sides.

After you are satisfied that the outline cut is in good order, proceed to the smoothing cut. Adjust the water flow to get a drop of water about every two seconds. Using the same 2 mm round bur and a very slow motor speed, begin to carefully smooth the outside edges of the outline cut. Except for the stem, the inside of the outline cut will be cut away later, so there is no point in smoothing the inside of the outline

cut. Wash the glass, dry it, and inspect for unwanted irregularities and chips on the outside of the outline cuts. Check your work again with the drawing and make corrections, if needed.

Cut the stem, using the same 2 mm round bur, to the same depth as the outline cut; use the same motor speed and water supply. The round bur makes a perfect stem in just a single line cut. Work the stem to the proper depth in a smooth, curving cut. Then smooth both edges with a slow motor speed.

The next step is to cut the inside of the petals. Use the same 2 mm round bur that you used to cut the outline. The water flow should be about one drop per second and the motor speed should be medium. Cut the petals that appear in

The petals and leaves are outlined and the stem is cut. (Engraving side)

The inside of the petals and center of the flower are cut. (Engraving side)

the background first; this allows for deeper cuts on petals in the foreground so that they will appear to overlap the other petals when seen from the viewing side of the glass. Start at the center of the tip end of the petal and make a cut lengthwise to the base of the petal. Make a second cut and a third cut on each side of the center cut, all at the same depth as the outline cut. Then, cut out all high spots between these cuts until you have a flat surface inside the petal. Complete all petals in this manner and smooth them, using a slow motor speed and little water. Now, chuck the 1 mm bur into the handpiece and, using a medium motor speed, deepen and define the edges of the petals that overlap other petals. Taper these cuts up to join the depth of the original cut. With a slow speed and less water, smooth the cuts just made. While you have the 1 mm bur in the handpiece, sharpen and touch up the tips of the petals.

You are now ready to engrave the center of the flower. It is simply a round, concave cut, about 1 mm deeper than the petals. Chuck the 4 mm round bur into the handpiece, adjust the water to a drop per second, and use a medium motor speed. Make the initial cut exactly on the scribed line that indicates the center area. Work this cut to about one-third the depth of the 4 mm round bur, and smooth the outer edges of the circle with a slow motor speed. Next, cut out the bulk inside of the outline. Continue with the 4 mm round bur with a medium-to-fast speed, and use a little more water. Make sure that the very center of the circle is a little deeper than the outline cut and make a smooth transition from the center out to the outline cut. Use the same 4 mm round bur for the smoothing cut, being careful to take out any rough or high spots.

The petals, center, and stem are now virtually completed, except for final details, which will be left until last. Cut the leaves to the same depth and in the same manner as the petals and carefully smooth them. After the leaves are cut, wash the glass and inspect your work again and make needed corrections. You are now ready to make the final touches to the engraving.

Switch, again, to the 1 mm round bur to cut the round dots that represent the stamens of the flower. With a water flow of one drop per second, use a slow motor speed and press the bur lightly as if drilling a hole. The bur will make a round indentation in the surface of the glass. Make the dots adjacent to one another all over the surface of the concave center of the flower. Touch up the tips of the leaves while you have the 1 mm round bur in the handpiece.

The final cuts are made with the 3/4 inch (19 mm) flat saw using the same water flow. These cuts represent the

The leaves are cut and the edges of the engraving is smoothed. (Engraving side)

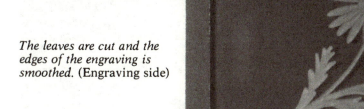

veins of the leaves. Make the cuts with a slow speed and use a light touch because the saw cuts very quickly. Draw a steady line with the saw in the center of the leaves from the base to the tips; these are the main veins. Then pencil in small lines representing the branch veins of the leaves. Now carefully cut these lines so that they connect with the main vein.

Wash and dry the glass, inspect it, and make any needed corrections. Then sign your name on the viewing side of the glass.

The basic cuts you have learned in these exercises will be used throughout all your engravings. You will be adding other sizes and shapes to your bur collection, learning how to use them, and developing your own techniques and methods. I would recommend that you continue with the flat glass, trying other subjects, before going on to the more expensive crystal. The decision is up to you as to when you are ready for the more sophisticated glass and subjects.

Veins are cut in the leaves and the stamens are cut in the center to finish the engraving. (Viewing side of the vase)

4

Choosing Glass Blanks and Designs to Engrave

GLASS BLANKS

A blank is glass that has no cuts or marks on the surface to be engraved. Any transparent, smooth, and polished glass can be used for engraving. However, I prefer clear, colorless glass because the frosted engraving shows to a greater advantage on it, whether lighted or not (colored glass almost always needs to be lighted).

If a painter needs canvas, board, or paper on which to apply his medium, it is a simple matter to go to an art supply store and choose from numerous sizes, textures, and qualities for his particular need. Not so with the glass engraver. I know of no glassmakers who design glass — other than for use by their own artisans — specifically for engravers. This leaves the individual engraver no choice but to seek out pieces from ready-made glass, wherever it can be found. Fortunately, glassmakers do turn out beautifully designed and undecorated pieces on which the engraver can put his design. It is usually more practical to design the subject to fit the glass than it is to find the glass to fit the subject.

Perhaps one of the most challenging things about engraving is finding the appropriate glass for a particular project. In some instances it is almost impossible, but continue searching anyway. Sometimes, just the right piece will turn up in the most unexpected place. A friend once found a set of heavy glass bookends at a garage sale and bought them for me. After the front and back surface had been ground and polished, they were great pieces to work with.

Once when my wife, Eddie, and I were browsing through a gift department of a large department store, my eye was immediately drawn to the sparkle of glass on a table with sale items. Sure enough! There were two crystal cubes, three inches square on the table. They were initialed blocks to be used as paper weights or decorative pieces. Each had a chipped corner, but I bought them at once for one dollar each — only a fraction of their regular price. I used one for an engraved celestial scene and incorporated the damaged spot into the design. The other one has the chipped part sawn off, using a diamond-edged saw, polished, and just waiting for an appropriate subject to become another work of art.

I point out these examples to impress upon you the advantage of keeping a sharp lookout wherever you are for glass that could be used for engraving.

Of course, the obvious and best places to look for glass are department stores and specialty shops that stock glassware, fine crystal, and china. Make a practice of hunting out small gift or antique shops in places you visit. Once in a while you may find a special bonus.

Beginners should purchase ordinary, inexpensive household glass bowls, vases, and plates for their first finished engravings before going on to the more expensive lead crystal glass.

Vases are the most available pieces on which to engrave, because almost all department and gift stores stock them. Fortunately, they are suited perfectly for the art. Choose vases that have relatively large, unobstructed areas on which to put your engraving designs, unless you wish to incorporate a small design or an initial on a vase that has a

A few of the many forms of glass blanks that are suitable for engraving.

Adam and Eve. Engraved vase. Nine inches high (22.86 cm). Collection of Mr. and Mrs. J. Robert Miller.

limited engraving area. As a general rule, though, be wary of a vase that is faceted. You can find vases that are round, oval, square, rectangular, hexagonal, octagonal, and in other shapes suitable for engraving. Sometimes the shape or design of the vase itself will inspire an idea for engraving.

The Swedish glass of Orrefors and Strömbergshyttan are excellent vases to use for engraving. Also, Val St. Lambert crystal, which is produced in Belgium, is very good quality to use. These vases are of fine lead crystal, with the wall thickness heavy enough for deep engraving, and they are available without cuts or decorations. You will find the names and addresses of the American importers in *Materials and Where to Obtain Them* in the back pages of this book. You can write to them for the names of retail distributors in your area. (Of course, there are many more brands of fine glass and lead crystal, both domestic and imported, that make vases suitable for engraving. The three that I mentioned are my favorites.) Always choose vases with walls that are thick enough, so that during the engraving process you do not engrave so deeply as to make the vase weak at that point. The minimum thickness should be about 1/4 inch (6.4 mm).

Three vases by Strömbergshyttan that are well suited for engraving. The wall thickness is 3/4 inch (19 mm). The vase heights, from left to right: 9 1/2 inches (23.2 cm), 10 1/2 inches (25.6 cm), and 8 inches (19.5 cm).

Fine lead crystal vases are expensive, but since you are going to spend hours executing an intricate design — after mastering the art — surely the outcome of your efforts should be reflected in the best of materials. Make it a habit to examine carefully for flaws and air bubbles in the glass when purchasing a vase. Lead glass is softer than plate glass and scratches more easily. This sometimes occurs in packing or unpacking, or clerks may be careless in handling at the store. Avoid pieces that are damaged unless the design you have in mind for that particular piece can cover the flaw. Tell the department head or store manager of your needs. Occasionally they have good crystal that has been slightly damaged in handling at bargain prices. Often it can be re-worked and polished to eliminate the damage or your design can disguise the flawed spot. Crystal bowls and plates are ideal pieces on which to engrave. Again, use the same criteria in selecting them as with the vases.

Crystal *objet d'art* pieces can sometimes be used to great advantage. For instance, a piece formed like a fish could be used to engrave a nautical motif. A crystal flower could have a butterfly engraved on it, and a glass ship would lend itself beautifully to a related engraved subject such as a mermaid. Crystal animals with relatively flat side surfaces can also be engraved.

You should take into consideration the distortion that can occur with abrupt changes in the contour of the glass and must allow for these distortions when planning the design unless, of course, you are working with a square vase, or bowl with straight sides, or a flat piece of glass. It would be difficult, for instance, to engrave a building from the extreme left side to the extreme right on a round vase and keep proper perspective, because the rounded contour of the vase would make curved lines out of all the straight ones. On the other hand, you could readily engrave a vertical tree trunk on the round glass without encountering the same problem. This is not to imply that round glasses or vases are limited only to slender trees or vertical subject designs, but to explain what can happen because of a change in the contour of the glass.

Decorative pieces, such as geometric forms, are exciting to work with. I discovered a prism that is ideal for engraving. It is a six-inch (15.24 cm) long, fine, flawless optical prism used in the sighting device of a tank. These prisms are available in army surplus stores as well as from Edmund Scientific Company (see *Materials and Where to Obtain Them*). I have been able to accumulate a collection of these, thanks to friends who have picked them up for me from all over the country. Amazing things happen when an engraving is placed on the right-angle sides of the prism and it is viewed from the face side. Cuts placed on one side are re-

Dragonfly. Irregularly shaped glass. Four inches high (10.16 cm). Collection of Shirle and A. J. Hoover.

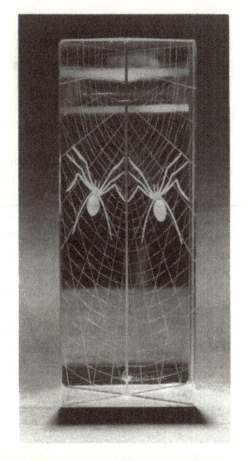

Distortion of the yardstick caused by the curvature of the glass at the edges of the vase. The same thing would happen to an engraving that extended from one side of the vase to the other. The oval vase on the left would accommodate a larger engraving, while the vase on the right could accept a vertical design to advantage.

Engraved prism with scribed lines as the spider's web. Collection of Mr. and Mrs. Steve Graham.

flected on the opposite side and appear to be behind cuts made on that side, giving great depth and added dimension to the creation. This phenomenon offers unlimited possibilities for design.

The housing has to be removed from around the prism and the sealant carefully pried away to gain access to the glass. Then the silvered mirror back is removed with a solution of 10% nitric acid as described below. You can buy the prisms either silvered on the face of the prism or with the silver removed. Since these are surplus items, some of the prisms may have slight chips at the corners. You have a choice of qualities at Edmund, with the better grades costing a little more. I prefer to order the ones that are silvered because they seem to be in a better condition.

The materials needed for removing silver from a prism are as follows:

10% solution of nitric acid
Plastic gloves
Goggles
Cotton swabs
Cradle to hold prism

The silver is removed with the acid solution. When working with the acid, use plastic gloves and goggles or glasses. To remove the silver, the prism should be held level, with the silvered side up, in a wooden cradle. The cradle can be made with two blocks of one-inch (25.4 mm) white pine measuring two inches (50.8 mm) by two inches (50.8 mm) with a V notch cut into one side of both pieces. The blocks are placed on a level surface, about four inches (10.16 cm) apart, with the V notch in the upright position. This should be placed on a plastic coffee can lid or plastic sheet to protect the work surface from the acid. Next, place the prism, with the silvered side up, into the notch of the blocks. Mix a solution of one part nitric acid to ten parts water. (Add the acid to wa-

Removing the silver surface from the face of a prism with a 10% solution of nitric acid.

ter, *never* water to the acid.) Better yet, have a pharmacist prepare the solution for you. Apply the acid solution to the prism with a long handled cotton swab. The silver will immediately disappear. Wash the prism, blocks, and lid thoroughly with water, dry, and store the blocks and lid for future use. It's a lot of work, but a lot of reward is gained.

There are other geometric pieces such as squares, rectangles, trapezoids, and pyramids that can be engraved. These can be paper weights or simply decorative pieces. Check with a specialty store or decorating gallery; if they do not have these in stock, perhaps they can order them for you.

Water glasses, wine glasses, and mugs are particularly well suited for stipple and scribe engraving because they are usually too thin to accept the deeper cuts of diamond bur engraving. The higher the lead content of the glass, the softer it is and the better for engraving. These glasses can be found in department and specialty stores.

MAKING GLASS BLANKS
Described below is the equipment used for making glass blanks. Though not necessary for the beginner, these tools

Diamond-saw unit. The one shown here is a ten inch (25.4 cm) saw. Larger sizes are available. Courtesy, Highland Park Manufacturing Company.

will prove useful later, should the student explore the art to its fullest:

Ten- or fourteen-inch (25.4 or 35.56 cm) diamond saw with motor
Eighteen-inch (45.72 cm) cast iron lap unit with motor
Water container device
Polishing arbor and six-inch (15.24 cm) polishing drum
Piece of 1/8 inch (3.17 mm) sheet cork, three inches (7.6 cm) by twenty four inches (60.96 cm)
Contact cement
Sixteen ounces (474 ml) number 280 grit silicon carbide abrasive
Sixteen ounces (474 ml) number 400 grit silicon carbide abrasive
Sixteen ounces (474 ml) number 600 grit silicon carbide abrasive
Eight ounces (237 ml) cerium oxide polishing powder
Four fruit jars for the abrasive and polishing powder
Three one-inch (25.4 mm) paint brushes
Three bowls for mixing the abrasive

The equipment described here is available from lapidary supply stores, and is more expensive than the basic tools required for engraving. It is used to fashion rough glass chunks into finished pieces, ready to engrave.

Eighteen inch (45.72 cm) cast
iron lap, used for cutting flat
planes on glass. Courtesy,
Lapidabrade, Inc.

Polishing arbor. Splash guards
are a necessity and are
available for polishing arbors.

Chunk of glass to be shaped, cut, and polished.

Look for chunks of glass in curio stores, gem and mineral shops, and at decorator studios. These glass chunks are usually the result of the glassmakers' periodic cleaning of their crucibles. It is apt to contain air bubbles or flaws, but is fun to work into polished blanks to engrave upon.

Always use goggles to protect your eyes when working with glass. First, we must have a way to cut the rough, jagged exterior into a reasonable shape. The diamond saw is used for this purpose. The circular saw blade itself has industrial-grade diamond bort imbedded in the metal at the periphery. It is mounted at the end of an arbor that is turned by a belt and pulley from an electric motor. The housing for the blade contains an oil coolant in which the blade revolves. Most saw units have a vise to hold the object to be sawn and a feeding mechanism to pull the object at the correct speed through the saw. I have a ten inch (25.4 cm) saw with a gravity feed vise that I use when practical; otherwise, I feed the glass through the saw with my hands. Wear gloves and be wary of glass slivers and sharp edges, should you try this, and always use goggles to protect the eyes when sawing.

When the glass is sawn to shape, the next step is to grind the surfaces smooth of the saw marks and prepare it for pol-

Using the diamond saw to cut the rough glass to shape.

The flat planes are ground smooth with the cast iron lap.

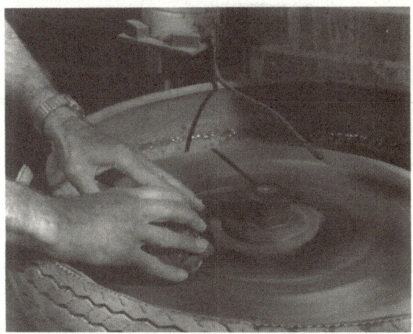

ishing. The surfaces of the glass are now ground flat on a lap, a circular disc of cast iron, eighteen inches (45.7 cm) in diameter and 1 1/4 inches (31.8mm) in thickness. It is powered by a one-half horsepower motor and revolves horizontally on a vertical shaft at about one hundred revolutions per minute. To use the lap, place the glass surface to be ground face down on the revolving lap. Apply a mixture of water and abrasive powder to the revolving lap to achieve the cutting. To drip water on the lap, as a coolant, I rigged a container from a coffee can with a valve soldered to the bottom edge to accommodate a 1/4 inch (6.4 mm) copper tubing that extends over the lap. Adjusting the valve to let a drop of water fall on the lap about every second keeps the abrasive slurry at the correct consistency and prevents the glass from becoming overheated enough to crack.

Number 280 grit silicon carbide abrasive is mixed with water to a creamy consistency in a bowl or other container and a one inch (25.4 mm) paint brush is used to apply the mix to the surface of the lap. Too much water dripping on the lap will cause the glass to glide over the abrasive without much cutting action; too little water and there is a danger of the glass grabbing the surface of the lap and jerking the glass out of your hands. A little experience is needed and you will learn the feel of when it is just right.

After all surfaces are ground flat with number 280 grit abrasive, the glass blank is washed thoroughly clean of the coarse grit. It is advisable to use a hand brush to clean grit from under your fingernails; if one tiny grain of the preceding size grit contaminates the succeeding finer grit, it can cause a bad scratch and the grinding sequence has to begin again. The next step is to cut the same surfaces in the same manner as before, but with a finer number 400 grit silicon carbide abrasive. Mix the 400 grit in another bowl and use a different brush to avoid contamination. Proceed to grind until all surfaces are finished. A good way to make sure that the entire surface has been ground is to crosshatch the surface

Polishing the flat planes, using cerium oxide on a cork-faced wheel.

with a pencil. When all the pencil lines are gone, you can assume that contact has been made over the entire cut.

Now, do the final prepolish cut with a finer 600 grit abrasive. Use the same procedure, taking care to clean the glass, lap, and your hands of the 400 grit. Again, use a separate container and brush for this final prepolishing grit. After you are satisfied that all facets of the glass have been ground with the finishing grit, wash everything thoroughly for final polishing.

This polishing is accomplished by the use of cerium oxide polishing powder on a cork wheel. I use a home-made arbor with a three-quarter horsepower motor. Commercial units are available in lapidary equipment stores, but to me, half the enjoyment of any project is making as much of the equipment as possible. The polishing wheel is a six inch (15.24 cm) diameter by three inches (7.62 cm) wide lapidary sanding drum. One-eighth inch (3.17 mm) cork sheeting was cut to the exact size of the drum face and glued to the surface with contact cement. The one-to-one pulley ratio turns the drum about 1750 rpm.

About two or three tablespoons of cerium oxide are

The finished piece, ready for engraving.

mixed with water to a thick, creamy consistency in a half-pint (237 ml) jar. The polishing compound is reuseable, so don't worry about mixing too much. The cork is wet and the polishing paste is applied with the fingers by dipping them in the paste and dabbing it.in spots over the surface. *Caution again*! Use goggles or glasses to protect your eyes and an apron to protect your clothes from the splatter. The glass is placed against the revolving wheel with moderate pressure and moved from side to side and up and down. When the wheel becomes dry, the motor is stopped, the cork wheel re-wet, more paste applied, and the polishing process begun again. The procedure is repeated until the glass is clear and shiny.

The glass is then washed, dried, and studied in a good light — outdoors in the sunlight, if possible. If there are hazy patches on the glass, the polishing is continued until they disappear. The glass is now ready for engraving.

MAKING CHIPPED EDGES

An interesting effect for glass engraving can be obtained by chipping the edges of the chosen piece to create a rough, yet crisp surface. This effect is especially good when accompanied by an appropriate design: a chipped edge can give the illusion of cresting waves for a sailing ship motif, or the tops of craggy mountains for a landscape design, for example.

The procedure for making the rough edge requires only a wood wedge and a hammer. The wedge should be about three inches (7.62 cm) long, one inch (25.4 mm) wide, and one-half inch (12.7 mm) in thickness. The lower half of its length should be tapered to a dull point. It should be made of hardwood, such as oak or hickory.

Exercise extreme precautions to protect eyes and hands from flying glass. Place the glass on a smooth wooden working surface, and hold the heel of one hand on the glass, with the wedge grasped between your thumb and forefinger. Place the point of the wedge on the face of the glass 1/8 inch (3.17 mm) from the edge and strike the wedge sharply with the hammer. Usually, a crescent-shaped chip will flake off the edge. Move the wedge to the side of the first chipped

The base of this engraving was cut to a rectangular shape and the edges chipped for an interesting effect. Collection of Dr. and Mrs. J. D. Magee.

place and repeat with another sharp blow, and so on, around the glass. Turn the glass over and treat the other side the same way until all the edges have been distressed in this manner. Native Americans used a similar method to fashion arrow heads from flint, using a piece of deer antler or hard bone as a wedge.

DESIGNS TO ENGRAVE
No matter what subject you choose to engrave, consideration should be given to the composition of the design and its eventual effect upon the particular glass on which it is to appear. Remember, you are usually working in reverse (on one side of the glass which is to be viewed from the other side) so always be aware of this reverse condition. For in-

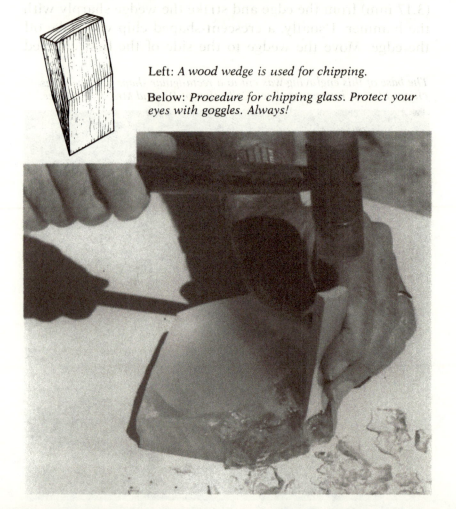

Left: *A wood wedge is used for chipping.*

Below: *Procedure for chipping glass. Protect your eyes with goggles. Always!*

The sailing-ship design was enhanced by chipping the edges of the glass to shape. Collection of the Author.

stance, the left hand of a person on the engraving side of the glass would appear as the right hand on the viewing side of the glass. Or, if you should engrave lettering on glass to be viewed from the opposite side, the letters would have to be reversed on the engraving side of the glass. One sure way to study the effect of a design on the glass is to roughly pencil it on the glass with a china marking pencil, then examine the results from the viewing side of the glass. The composition and correctness of the design will become apparent before the design is finalized.

Another item to be considered is the contour of the glass to be engraved. For example, if you were to plan an engraving of a tree trunk on a small round vase, the tree trunk would appear thinner from the viewing side due to the concave shape of the vase. The remedy would be to make the tree trunk wider than usual so that it would appear to be normal when seen from the viewing side of the vase.

Composition plays an important role in engraving. Plan your engraving as an artist plans a painting. Be sure that the elements of the engraving are pleasing in size and arrangement on the glass that is to be used. Again, use the china marking pencil and draw your design on the glass to check the composition from the viewing side of the glass. If the design doesn't seem to be correct for this particular piece of glass, simply wash off the pencil marks and try again. No damage has been done to the glass.

Almost everything that can be drawn can be engraved. Figures of flowers, trees, animals, people, insects, and geometric designs are all readily cut into glass. As stated before, trees are one of my favorites, and there are an endless variety of species, shapes, and sizes. Delicate butterflies are a challenge and are popular and appealing to almost everyone. Other insects are often very interesting to depict in certain situations. Flowers and their leaves are irresistible. Graceful deer and some of the more exotic animals are fun to do. Birds make fine subjects, too.

Perhaps you could illustrate a figure from one of your favorite poems, plays, or stories in glass. These make classical pieces that will stay popular forever. Fish and sea shells and boats are good subjects. Geometric and abstract designs are especially suited to vases with limited flat planes.

Where do you find pictures of these subjects for reference? Simple! Go through discarded magazines, catalogs, and other publications, clip pictures of the nature of subject you wish to engrave, then file them alphabetically. The public library usually has available current and back issues of a wide variety of magazines. The library is a wonderful source for material. They usually have a copy machine available. However, it is good to have your sketch book handy. Books on natural history and the inexpensive paperback art books found at art supply stores are excellent sources.

Use your reference guide with discretion. Do not get too literal and copy the subject exactly; rather, interpret it your own way. Glass engraving is a self-expressive art, and you will want to create your own designs with individuality. I feel there are great unexplored opportunities to engrave designs on baroque and extremely contoured glass, turning the disadvantage of distortion into an asset by creating unusual optical effects. Abstract designs, too, hold unlimited challenges to express new ideas in this versatile medium. The subject matter, the technique, and the medium itself presents infinite possibilities.

What subject should you use for a particular piece of glass? Study the glass. Does its shape bring anything to mind? Do the qualities of the glass itself project a meaning? The decision is yours to make. That is the fun and the creative freedom of glass engraving.

❦

5

ENGRAVING A VASE: DEMONSTRATION

The purpose of this demonstration is to acquaint you with the proper use of the tools and procedures used in completing a glass engraving. Although this project is a bit advanced for the beginner, it is given here as an example of what can be accomplished after proficiency is gained through practice.

I selected a vase that is well suited for engraving and a subject that will involve the use of a variety of diamond burs. The engraving is executed intaglio on the back outside surface of the vase, opposite the final viewing side. With the exception of subject matter and the fact that the viewer will be looking through the front wall of the vase, the engraving will be done in the same manner as the exercises in chapter 2.

The owl design is engraved on a beautiful crystal vase. The vase is rather flat in shape and measures seven inches (17.78 cm) high, six inches (15.24 cm) across, and three inches (7.62 cm) deep. The glass is about 3/4 inch (19 mm) thick, which affords plenty of depth to cut as deeply as needed. The back and front are gently curved and free of distortion. The vase is comparatively free of bubbles and swirls, as is the case with all fine crystal. Note that, as a beginner, you should use the flat practice glass until you feel completely confident about going on to engraving expensive crystal! Even after you gain some experience it would be wise to do the intended design on practice glass before engraving it on crystal.

The burs used for this engraving demonstration are:

1/2 mm round bur
1 mm round bur
2 mm round bur
4 mm round bur
10 mm round bur
12 mm round-edge wheel bur
6 mm inverted tapered cylinder bur
1 mm flame-shaped bur
12 mm barrel-shaped bur
8 mm flat saw
3/4 inch (19 mm) Cratex wheel

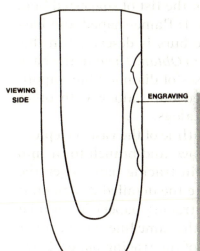

VIEWING SIDE

ENGRAVING

Left: *Cross-section drawing of vase, showing the engraving side in relation to the viewing side.*

Below: *The blank crystal vase, seven inches (17.78 cm) high.*

Outline drawing of vase and design on tracing paper.

Note that there are two diamond burs used in the owl engraving that are not included in the list of suggested burs for the beginner given in chapter 1: flame-shaped and barrel-shaped burs. The use of these burs is described in this chapter. See *Materials and Where to Obtain Them* in the back pages of this book for the addresses of diamond bur suppliers. The flame- and barrel-shaped burs, along with other shapes, will be shown in their catalogs.

The first step is to draw the outline of the vase on a piece of drawing paper and sketch the owl and branch to fit into the outline. Placing a piece of thin tracing paper over the sketch, trace the owl and complete the detailed design on it (side one, or viewing side, of the tracing paper). Then turn the tracing paper over and pencil the same lines on the other side (side two, or engraving side) of the tracing paper. Now, there is a complete drawing of the pattern on both sides of the tracing paper. Place the vase on the worktable directly in front of you; it should always be placed on a cloth to avoid scratches on the soft lead crystal. Now position side one of the tracing toward the glass on the back outside of the vase and tape it securely with masking tape; this is the way the

The drawing is taped to the vase and transferred to the glass. (Viewing side of vase)

finished engraving will be viewed. Remember, the work is done on the opposite side of the vase from the viewing side, so you must be sure to check to see that the design is turned the correct way. A piece of carbon paper is slipped between the tracing paper and the glass, then a hard lead pencil is used on the tracing to transfer the pattern design to the glass. Scribe the outline of the design with the diamond pencil, just inside the transferred carbon lines.

The design is scribed on the vase with the diamond pencil. (Engraving side of vase)

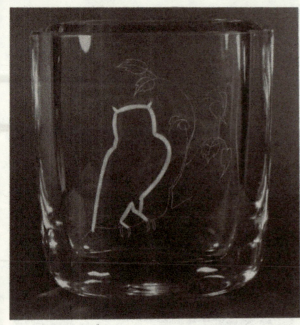

Begin the first engraved outline using a round bur. (Engraving side of vase)

Now that the guidelines are scribed on the glass, tape the original drawing, engraving side out, to the wall in front of you and chuck a 4 mm round bur into the handpiece; turn on the water to one drop per second (for all cutting). Start a cut directly on the scribed line, outlining the body of the owl. This cut should be made to about the depth of one-third of the diameter of the bur and then carefully smoothed.

Body of owl and main limbs are cut. (Engraving side of vase)

Check your work after each cut by turning the vase to the viewing side. Exchange the 4 mm bur for a 2 mm round and cut the outline for the "ears" (feathers) and legs.

The next step is to cut in the body of the owl. Use a fast-cutting 12 mm round-edge wheel and plenty of water. When the body is roughed out to about 1/4 inch (6.4 mm) deep, cut the limb on which the owl is sitting, using the 4 mm round bur; smooth the edges with this same bur. Make the cut for the limb fairly shallow, because — and this is very important — the owl's feet will have to appear to be clutching the limb. If the limb is cut too deep, the feet will have to be cut deeper and distortion and an imbalance of depth will occur. Notice that the owl's tail feathers go behind the limb, so they will need to be cut shallowly to keep perspective in balance. In other words, if the limb, feet, and tail feathers are cut too deep, they would appear to be forward of the owl's body when viewed from the front of the vase. In reality, if the owl is to keep itself upright on the limb, its feet must be tucked under, with its breast protruding forward. Keep perspective and balance in mind for all of your engravings, just as if you were modeling in clay.

VIEWING
SIDE

ENGRAVING
SIDE

View of the owl's profile. Dotted lines show depth of the feet in relation to the depth of the owl's breast.

The branch extending vertically beside the owl is cut, starting with a 2 mm round bur at the base, then the 1 mm round is used as the branch is tapered. The 6 mm flat saw is used for the smaller twigs.

Once the body of the owl is completely cut, use a regular graphite drawing pencil on the ground glass to draw in the features as a guide to cut by. Carefully do this by using the

he wings and the main limb re cut deeper, and the bark exture is added to the limb. Engraving side of vase)

original drawing as a reference. Cut the wings deeper than the body, using the 12 mm round-edge wheel and the 10 mm round bur. At the point where the leading edge of the owl's left wing overlaps the body, use an inverted tapered cylinder to achieve the abrupt protrusion. Next, the right wing is cut, using a 4 mm round bur; it is then smoothed with the same bur.

In profile, the owl's breast protrudes in relation to the body, so cut this area deeper, tapering to a more shallow cut from the breast to the head and downward from the breast to the legs. A 12 mm round-edge wheel and the 12 mm barrel-shaped sintered bur are used to smooth the body. Now work the tail feathers almost to completion, being careful not to cut too deeply.

The head is next. Using a 10 mm round bur, continue to round out and smooth the concave head, checking from the viewing side of the vase for depth and shape. When these are satisfactory, start at the V of the brow, just above the beak. Again, for this sharp angle, use the inverted tapered cylinder and gradually deepen the cut toward the "ears" at the top of each side of the head. Switch to a 1-mm round bur to smooth any spots left by the previous bur and to put the point on the "ears."

The beak is cut at the base with a 2 mm round bur and gradually cut in toward the point with a 1 mm one. Finish the very tip with a small flame-shaped bur. Remember, you are cutting the beak in so that, when viewed from the other side, it will appear to come out toward the viewer.

Use the 1 mm round bur to cut a line from the beak, around the eyes, up to the brow; this indicates the edge of the semicircle of feathers that ring the eyes. Use the same bur to cut rays from the eyes to the edge of the circle to represent these feathers. Finally, cut the eyes in with a round bur, gradually widening a circle until the diameter of the eyes match the original drawing. As a finishing touch on the owl's face, use a 3/4 inch (19 mm) Cratex wheel (see page 109) to semipolish the eyes; this gives a luminous quality to

The feathers are carved, more detail is added to the owl, and the eyes are semi-polished with the Cratex wheel. (Engraving side of vase)

them when the vase is displayed against a dark background.

At this point, wash the vase, carefully dry it with a paper towel or soft cloth, and study the work done so far. I do this, periodically, throughout the engraving process. The break rests my eyes, helps me to evaluate my next step, and, if I get impatient to go on with the engraving, to avoid mistakes. I never finish an engraving in one sitting. The engraving described here will take many work sessions and literally hours to complete.

Now, let's go back to the limb: this is worked to completion, using the inverted tapered cylinder to texture the bark, as we did in the practice exercise. In this step the limb is cut more shallowly than it was before and it terminates with a soft irregular line. The smaller end of the limb is broken, with a jagged termination.

The legs of the owl are feathered and the feet are cut deeper into the limb with 1 mm and 2 mm round burs. The scales of the lower legs and feet are cut with a very small inverted cone.

Use a pencil, again, on the engraving side of the glass to detail the position of the feathers, using side two of the original drawing as a guide. Then, with the 1 mm round bur, cut in all the feathers on the wings and body and texture them with a 1/2 mm round bur.

With the owl and limb practically finished, it is time to add the leaves to the branches. Outline each leaf lightly with a 1 mm round bur, then cut the bulk out and form the leaves with 2 mm and 4 mm round burs. The 8 mm flat saw is used to cut the sharp points on the leaves. Finish the leaves by carefully smoothing them with the 4 mm round bur.

It is time to clean the vase and see how it looks. Taking the vase to the sink and placing the foam rubber pad from the catching pan on the bottom of the sink to protect the soft crystal, wash it with detergent and a soft cloth. Now, dry it carefully and study it for any missing details. Administer any final touch-ups and then sign and date it on the viewing side with the diamond pencil.

The engraving is finished.

The leaves are added to finish the engraving. The finished vase is in the collection of Mr and Mrs. Kent Morgan.
(Viewing side of vase)

6

OTHER TECHNIQUES AND TOOLS

DIAMOND POINT ENGRAVING

One of the oldest known forms of glass engraving was practiced by the ancient Romans. They inscribed designs on vases and drinking vessels with a hard, sharp stone — probably of flint. Records show that no serious attempts were made between this era and the sixteenth and seventeenth centuries to decorate glass by scribing. English engravers, at about the mid-sixteenth century, took a rather bold approach with their techniques. Using diamond point tools, they would outline their subjects with broad lines and fill in with straight and crosshatched lines to make flat patterns. Perhaps the zenith of diamond point engraving was reached in the eighteenth century by Dutch and English engravers who used the stipple method. These skilled artists created landscapes, still life, and portraits to a depth and beauty that almost defy description. One of the finest collections of stippled glass can be seen at the Victoria and Albert Museum in London. Stipple engraving is still being practiced, chiefly in England, where artists are producing some outstanding work.

Stipple engraving is a departure from the bas-relief effect achieved by engraving intaglio with diamond burs. In the stipple method, a diamond point or a steel scriber is used to scratch lines and tap dots into the surface of the glass to create form with highlights and shadows. This technique is similar to pen-and-ink or pencil drawings done on paper.

As opposed to diamond bur engraving, stipple and scribe engraving with a diamond pencil is generally done on the surface facing the viewer. I say generally, because there are exceptions to both engraving and stipple or scribe methods. A diamond bur engraving may appear on the front surface to create a special effect, and, by the same token, a stipple engraver may wish to engrave on the back surface for the same reason. For instance, an engraver can stipple or scribe a distant mountain landscape on the back side of a vase (away from the viewer) and scribe or stipple trees on the front side (facing the viewer), thereby giving the illusion of great depth. The scribe and stipple techniques can be used independently or together.

You should always wear goggles or glasses and mask as a precaution when stippling glass to protect your eyes and lungs from the small flying glass chips. Also, be aware that glass chips can be irritating to the hands, so keep the surface of the work area clean.

The use of the diamond pencil is the least expensive method of engraving glass. All that is needed is a piece of glass and a diamond pencil or a tungsten carbide steel scriber. However, the superior performance of the diamond is well worth the small additional cost.

Diamond point engraving techniques are many and varied. Each artist has his own way of personalizing his art, whether stipple, line, or a combination of both. The stipple method is accomplished by holding the diamond pencil in a vertical position and tapping close dots to create a form. The closer the dots, the lighter the area appears. When the dots are spaced farther apart, a shadowed or receding ap-

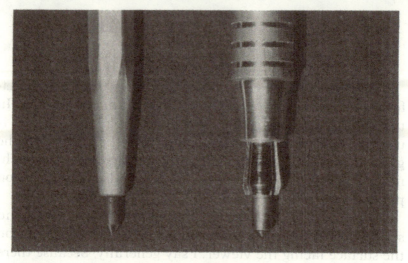

Magnified view of the scribers. On the left is a tungsten carbide steel scriber and on the right is a 90-degree-angle diamond scriber.

pearance is attained. Perhaps the best way to understand the technique is to use a ten or fifteen power magnifier to look at a photograph that has been reproduced in the newspaper. Notice that in the lighter areas the dots are smaller and appear to be farther apart, while, in the darker areas,

Using the diamond pencil to scribe and stipple a fish design on a mug. The black cloth inside the mug is used as a visual aid.

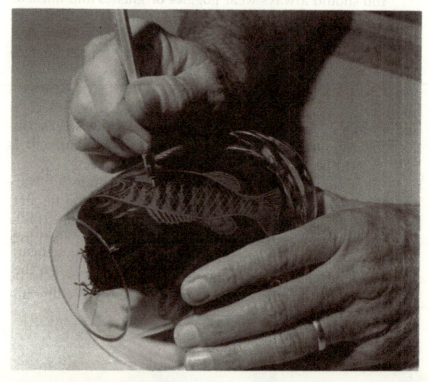

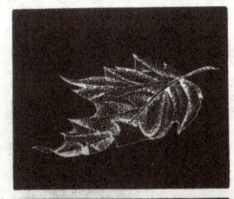

Drawing simulating the stipple technique. Spacing of dots creates form.

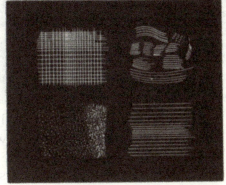

Practice exercises with the diamond scriber.

the dots are larger and appear to be closer. Since glass is a transparent medium, the principle applies in reverse when the dots are viewed against a dark background: close dots form a lighter area, while widely spaced dots become shadow areas. Good stipple engraving is a very controlled technique; the dots are not tapped out at random — they are carefully spaced.

For practice, you should again use any piece of plate glass. The glass can be thinner than that used for bur engraving because only the surface is disturbed. Do not use too much vigor with the diamond tool because the point can be shattered and ruined, and, on very thin glass, you might shatter the piece you are attempting to engrave. Try tapping the dots at close intervals but don't let them touch each other, and practice scribing short and long lines in the same

Diamond-point stipple and scribed design on a glass.

manner. Do some short curved lines and crosshatching. Use the diamond with a light touch when crosshatching because, as one line crosses another, the point dropping down into the valley of the first line causes stress on the point; this could result in damage to the diamond.

Now that you have the feel of the diamond pencil, try scribing your own design on a parfait or small wine glass. Work out your design carefully in pencil on a piece of paper, then copy the design on the glass with a china marking pencil. Do not make your design too complicated for your first try; birds, butterflies, flowers, and leaves are good subjects. Outline the design with the diamond, then rub off the pencil marks. A dark cloth stuffed inside the glass will help you to see the work better. Hold the glass in one hand and use the pencil in the other. Start filling in the detail, texture, and form with stipple, scribed lines, crosshatching, or a combination of all these. The technique is up to you. You will eventually develop your own style and look.

There will be occasions when you need to scribe or engrave a level line around the circumference of a vase or glass. To make the guideline, place a dot with a china marking pencil where you want the line on the glass. Set the glass upright on a table or flat level surface and stack books by the side of the glass to the height of the desired line. Place the china marking pencil on top of the books, with the point of the pencil touching the glass. Then, adjust up or down by adding or taking away from the stack of books until the point of the pencil is at the dot where the line is to be drawn. With one hand holding the pencil firmly against the glass, rotate the glass with the other hand, making a perfectly level and straight line around the glass. A pair of sculptors' calipers (an instrument with two legs, usually curved, held together with a rivet or screw) is helpful for measuring diameters and heights. These can be purchased at art supply stores.

For scribing straight lines on curved surfaces, you can make a plastic straightedge. Buy a piece of 1/16 inch (3.2 mm) thick acrylic sheeting from a plate glass supply store and cut a strip 1/2 inch (12.7 mm) wide by six inches (15.24 cm) in length. Sand the edges smooth: place a sheet of number 280 grit sandpaper on a perfectly flat table, stand the plastic strip vertically on edge lengthwise, and rub it back

Marking a level line around a vase. The china marking pencil is held against the vase while the vase is rotated with the other hand.

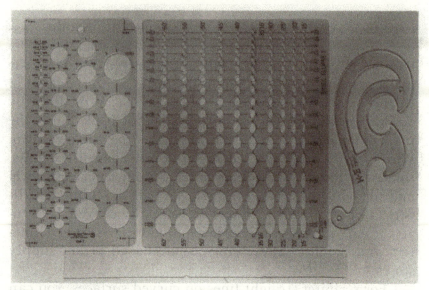

Ellipse and circle templates, irregular curves, and straightedge are used as aids in scribing precise lines.

and forth on the sandpaper until the edge is straight and smooth. When finished, the thin strip of plastic is very flexible and you can hold it to the contour of the glass with one hand while scribing with the other. Other aids for scribing precise lines are ellipse and circle templates and irregular curves, which you can purchase from an art supply store.

The art of stipple engraving is an exciting and challenging one. Each piece that you finish generates an idea for a different technique on the next one. Chances are that you will be pleasantly surprised when you view your finished piece against a dark background. Beautiful, isn't it? There is no medium quite like fine glass! It has dignified beauty all its own.

SUPPLEMENTAL TOOLS AND THEIR USE
We have already discussed the basic tools and their uses; now we will talk about some additional tools that you may wish to try.

Mizzy Wheel
The Mizzy Heatless Wheels are grinding wheels, one inch (25.4 mm) in diameter, made of silicon carbide. They are

Mizzy wheels. Fast-cutting wheels made of silicon carbide.

available in thicknesses of 3/32 inch (2.3 mm) and 1/8 inch (3.17 mm). Coarse and fast cutting, they are primarily used to rough out large areas. These wheels do not come mounted; to do this use a screw on a 1/8 inch (3.17 mm) mandrel. The Mizzy Wheels wear away rather quickly, but they are not expensive. Use plenty of water and be prepared to contend with an abundance of splattering slurry.

Diamond Core Drill
The diamond core drill is used for drilling holes in hard mineral materials. It is made of round steel tubing with a 1/4 inch (6.4 mm) shank at one end for chucking; the other end is

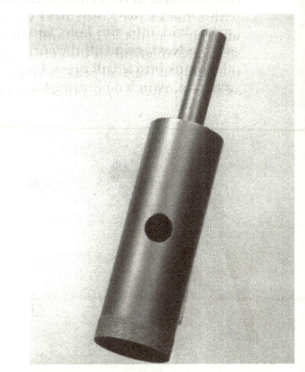

Diamond core drill.

diamond-impregnated for cutting. The wall thickness of the tubing is about 1/32 inch (.77 mm). Core drills are usually available in sizes 1/4 to 1 inch (6.4 mm to 25.4 mm) in diameter. They are useful in drilling holes and making perfect circular cuts in glass. They cannot be used with the handpiece, only with a drill press.

Copper Wheel

Using these small copper wheels should not be confused with regular copperwheel engraving, which requires a lathe, as described in chapter 2. Although the same principle of using oil and abrasive applies, these small copper wheels are chucked into the handpiece and are used much like the diamond bur. The copper wheel cuts more slowly than the diamond does, but makes a smoother cut. No water is required in this procedure. Use a slow speed and light touch.

Small copper wheels are not available commercially. However, if you wish to try them, a machinist can make them for you or you can make them yourself. Get a small sheet of copper about 1/8 inch (3.17 mm) thick and scribe a circle on it 1/4 inch (6.4 mm) in diameter. Drill a 3/32 inch (2.3 mm) hole at the center of the circle and cut out the circle with a hack saw. Now insert the shank of a 3/32 inch (2.3 mm) drill into the hole and the copper disc to the steel shank. Next, grind off the cutting part of the drill and chuck the shank into a drill press. Using a file, with a block of wood as a rest, switch on the press and start truing the copper into

Copper wheels.

a perfectly round disc. Still using the file, bevel both edges of the disc to a sharp edge. Use any angle bevel to suit the purpose of the cut.

I have made several of these small copper wheels in different thicknesses and cutting edges. I use them for very small lines, for cutting leaves, and other delicate cuts when diamond bur engraving.

To use the copper wheel, mix a small quantity of 400 grit silicon carbide grinding powder with a few drops of cutting oil until it becomes a thin paste. With the wheel chucked into the handpiece, dip the edge of the wheel into the mixture and bring it into contact with the glass. When the wheel stops cutting, dip it into the paste again. The grit will gradually imbed itself into the copper surface to form the cutting tool.

I would suggest that you try the copper wheel, if for no other reason than to learn the principle of copperwheel engraving and to find out how early wheel engravers worked.

Cratex Wheel
The Cratex is a rubber bonded abrasive wheel used in industry for fine sanding and finishing. They are available in 7/8 inch (22.19 mm) diameter wheels, knife-edge wheels, and

Cratex rubber bonded abrasive wheels.

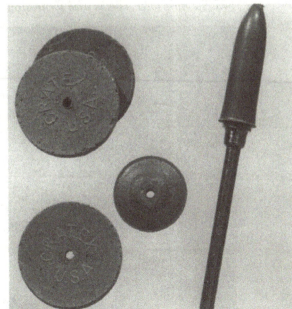

bullet shapes. There is a choice of extra fine, fine, medium, and coarse cutting abrasives. The operator should wear a mask or respirator when using Cratex wheels to avoid inhaling abrasive and silica dust.

I use the medium grade for semipolishing small areas in an engraving, for instance in putting the spots on a giraffe or the stripes on a zebra. They can be used anyplace on the engraving to indicate a change in color or texture. The Cratex wheel smooths the area, giving a darker appearance to that spot.

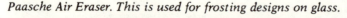

Air Eraser

This miniature sandblasting gun is called the Air Eraser for the simple reason that it is primarily used to erase pencil and ink from drawings with a jet of abrasive propelled by air. It is also used in industry for many other purposes. Our purpose is to frost areas and designs that are not to be engraved deeper on the glass.

The Air Eraser is a hand-held instrument with a container on top into which aluminum oxide abrasive powder is poured. The powder is fed into the nozzle, from which it is forced out in a jet of air to its target. About fifty pounds of air pressure from a regulated tank or air compressor is need-

Paasche Air Eraser. This is used for frosting designs on glass.

Crystal plate with inscription and leaf design done with the Air Eraser. The center design was engraved with diamond burs. Courtesy, Tittle, Luther, Loving, Architects. Engraving by the Author.

ed for working on glass. Some sort of enclosure, such as a cardboard box, should be used to contain the flying dust. Wear a respirator when working with the abrasive gun.

The unit can be used to frost vignette areas, which shade off gradually into the surrounding background, and to apply surface designs on glass. Masking tape and paper are used to protect areas not to be frosted. Air abrasive is an excellent way to letter on glass, using the method described here. Purchase a sheet of frisket (a thin, self-adhering, paper-backed film used by commercial artists to mask out areas on photographs and artwork when using an air brush) from an art supply store. The idea is to adhere the film to the glass, and then cut out and peel off the portion that is to be frosted. The remaining film acts as a mask, protecting the clear glass.

The design or lettering is drawn on paper as a guide, the frisket is taped over this with the film side up, and the design traced on the frisket with ink. The paper backing is peeled from the film and the film is adhered to the glass.

Frisket, with the design drawn on it, adhered to the glass.

Using a razor blade or X-acto knife, the design is cut through the film and peeled off the glass. Masking tape is used to protect the surrounding glass. Next, the Air Eraser is loaded with abrasive, and the pressure set at fifty pounds. The abrasive is directed toward the glass, which is about four inches (10.16 cm) from the nozzle of the gun. It only takes a few

Frisket is peeled off, exposing area to be frosted.

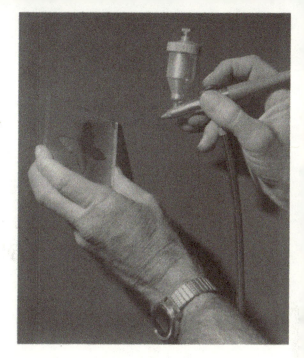

The Air Eraser is held about four inches (10.16 cm) from the glass, with the abrasive spray directed at the area to be frosted.

bursts from the abrasive to frost the design completely. Remove the mask, wash the glass, and you will see a perfectly frosted design on the glass.

The Air Eraser can be used to put a completed design on glass or, in conjunction with diamond bur engraving, to frost surface areas on the design.

The finished design after removing the frisket mask.

7

DISPLAYING YOUR WORK

In order to show glass engravings at their best, careful consideration should be given to selecting a proper setting. I once saw a display of fine, engraved glass that was sitting row upon row, side by side, on tables in the center of the room in a large museum. There was no apparent attempt to make an orderly arrangement of the pieces or even an artistically inviting display of the glass. This was a permanent collection of the museum. The display would have been so much more effective if some effort had been made in arrangement, background, and lighting.

Generally, engraved glass should be displayed in front of a dark background, with appropriate lighting on the glass to highlight the engraving. Glass that is to be used should be stored with and given the same care as other crystal. Heavier pieces, such as bowls, decanters, and vases, can be placed on tables or shelves, but to show your engravings at their best, they should be displayed and lighted properly. The following are some suggested ways for displaying engraved glass.

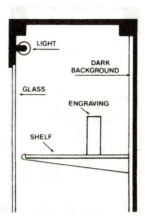

Cabinet design for displaying glass engravings. The light source is in front of and above the engraving.

CABINET WITH DIRECT LIGHTING

Glass-front cabinets with built-in lighting can be purchased from furniture stores. The cabinets usually have three or four glass shelves, and in some models the shelves are adjustable. The light, either incandescent or fluorescent, is placed in the front, above the glass door, on the inside of the cabinet. The top glass shelves do not interfere with the lighting on the lower shelves, so you can use all shelves by staggering the placement of the engraved glass from shelf to shelf. You may wish to drape black or dark-colored velvet on the inside back of the cabinet, or to cover the background with a matte black paint.

CABINET WITH INDIRECT LIGHTING

You will probably not find this type of cabinet on the market, but the cabinet described above could be modified, or one could be built by a cabinetmaker. For this display cabinet, the light is incandescent or fluorescent and is located in the bottom of the cabinet. A 1/4 inch (6.4 mm) opal glass (a strong, heat-resistant, white, translucent glass) shelf is placed above the light. The engravings sit on the opal glass shelf, thus illuminating the inside and outside of each piece

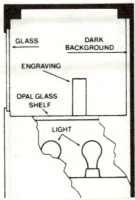

GLASS

DARK
BACKGROUND

ENGRAVING

OPAL GLASS
SHELF

LIGHT

Display cabinet with the light source beneath the translucent opal glass shelf.

in a pleasing bath of soft light. One could use the cabinet with direct lighting from above to create a sparkle effect on the outside of the glass and construct the indirect system below, thereby utilizing both types in one cabinet. The indirect lighting from below gives a soft luminous quality to the engraved glass.

SHADOW BOX DISPLAY

The shadow box is an excellent way to display and protect an engraving. It can be a small, wall hanging type or, should you have the courage to cut a hole into the wall of a room, a built-in one. In the built-in type, the shadow box is constructed of plywood with a picture frame molding for the front. The box can be any size in depth, depending upon the thickness of the wall and how far into the room you wish the box to protrude. It is usually limited to the space between the studs inside the wall, though a seasoned carpenter could construct one of larger dimensions by reinforcing the studs below and above an area being converted to a lighted shadow box display.

Inside is an opal glass shelf, supported by cleats that are placed 3 1/2 inches (8.89 cm) from the bottom of the box. A light socket is secured to the side of the box, below the glass shelf. Several 1/4 inch (6.4 mm) holes are drilled in the bot-

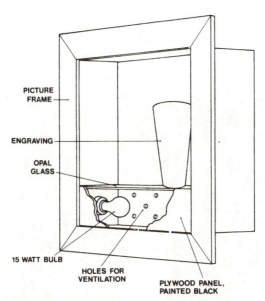

PICTURE
FRAME

ENGRAVING

OPAL
GLASS

15 WATT BULB

HOLES FOR
VENTILATION

PLYWOOD PANEL,
PAINTED BLACK

Diagram of the shadow box display. Made of 3/8 inch (9.5 mm) plywood, picture frame molding, and a 1/4 inch (6.4 mm) opal glass shelf.

tom and the back of the box, below the glass shelf, for ventilation. A 15 watt incandescent bulb is used for illumination; this can be fitted with an on-off switch on the cord that plugs into the electrical outlet. All of the interior of the box is covered with a black matte paint or material. The box is recessed into the wall, with only the picture frame front being visible on the room wall. If a glass front is used, you could hinge the picture frame so that changing the light bulb could be accomplished without removing the box from the wall. Without a glass front, it simply becomes a recessed, illuminated shelf with a picture frame front. After plugging in the light, the engraving or engravings are placed on the opal glass shelf, and a beautiful, three-dimensional picture is created! See the accompanying diagram for details of how the shadow box is constructed.

LIGHT BOX

Another way to show your work to good advantage is by using a light box. These light boxes can be obtained from Ana-

Light box displaying glass engraving. These boxes are available in several sizes. This engraving is in the collection of Mr. and Mrs. W. O. Sullivan.

lite, Inc. (see *Materials and Where to Obtain Them*) and are made for this particular purpose. The boxes are available in both square and round shapes, in sizes from four to eight inches (10.16 to 20.32 cm). For the very best results, cut a piece of picture framing glass the size of the top of the light box, cover it with self-adhesive black velour paper, which can be obtained at art and craft shops, set the engraving on this, and draw the outline of it with a white pencil. Then using a razor blade, cut a hole the exact size of the piece being displayed. When the engraved piece is placed on the cut-out spot, the light only shows through the piece; thus the engraving bursts into prominence with a soft glow that shows all the details of shading. Various size light boxes can

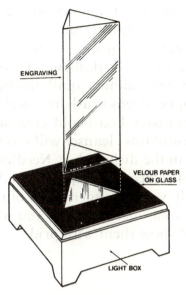

ENGRAVING

VELOUR PAPER ON GLASS

LIGHT BOX

The top for the light box is made of picture glass, cut to the exact size of the light box. Black adhesive velour paper is attached to the glass and the shape for the engraving base is cut from the velour.

be made by your local carpenter or cabinetmaker to accommodate larger pieces. The glass top may be recessed to fit flush with the top edge of the box.

I have used these light boxes successfully in shows by draping the background with deep maroon or dark blue silk velvet (it drapes better than cotton velvet). In an area where the light is subdued, with only the light emitting from the boxes through the glass engravings and reflecting on the velvet, it is a most exciting display, indeed!

THE CARE OF ENGRAVED GLASS

To show your engravings at their best, the glass must be kept clean. Use a mild detergent with warm water to make a sudsy bath and wash them by hand. Put a piece of one inch (25 mm) foam rubber or several layers of bath towel in the bottom of the sink or on the cabinet as a safety measure in case the glass slips from your hands while washing. Rinse the glass with warm water and dry with a soft towel. Use a pair of cotton gloves to transfer the glass to the display area. This avoids leaving fingerprints. If there are specks of lint remaining on the glass, whisk them off with a soft brush. I use a number 18 sign painters' quill brush, or you can purchase a photographers' lens brush from a photo supply store.

Never use abrasive household cleanser to wash your glass; repeated use of this cleanser will scratch it. Do not put engraved pieces in the dishwasher. Needless to say, display your work in a safe place and keep it out of the reach of small children. After all, you have spent a lot of time and worked hard to produce your engravings, so you want to take good care of them and show them with pride.

In Closing

The challenge of transforming a fine, pure piece of glass into a work of art is just as intriguing today as it was thousands of years ago. With today's modern equipment, the results can be accomplished effectively with much less effort than in the past.

Glass engraving not only satisfies a creative urge, it is also an expansion of your own artistic horizons. Your pleasures will range from that of simply enjoying a craftsperson's hobby to the sincere pleasure of accomplishing a valuable learning experience, and may lead to a satisfying occupation.

The examples shown in this book are the results of practical application and years of experience. I hope they will encourage you to develop your own skills and techniques. I assure you that you will be delighted with the results, regardless of your past artistic endeavors. Just keep the basic fundamentals in mind. Your personal ideas and innovations will make your work uniquely outstanding.

As you become proficient in the art of glass engraving, you will realize the unlimited challenges it offers!

If this book should in any small way encourage you to learn and continue the art of glass engraving or motivate you to a greater appreciation of an ancient and long-neglected, beautiful art form, then my efforts in preparing this book will be justly rewarded.

Materials and Where to Obtain Them

Motors, Handpieces
Foredom Electric Company,
  Inc.
Bethel, CT 06801

Swest, Inc.
11090 North Stemmons
Dallas, TX 75229

Diamond Burs
Diamond-Pro Unlimited
Box 25
Monterey Park, CA 91754

Diamond Scribers
Lunzer Industrial
  Diamonds, Inc.
48 West 48th Street
New York, NY 10036

Magnifiers
Donegan Optical Company,
  Inc.
14308 Lenexa, KS 66215

Diamond Pacific Tool
  Corporation
24063 West Main Street
Barstow, CA 92311

Laps, Polishing Units, Abrasives
Crown Manufacturing
  Company
926 Bing Street
San Carlos, CA 94070

Lapidabrade, Inc.
8 East Eagle Road
Havertown, PA 19083

Air Eraser
Paasche Airbrush Company
7440 West Lawrence Avenue
Harwood Heights, IL 60656

Light Boxes
Analite, Inc.
24 Newtown Plaza
Plainview, NY 11803

Prisms
Edmund Scientific Company
101 East Gloucester Pike
Barrington, NJ 08007

*Other supplies can be
obtained at lapidary shops.*

Suggested Reading:
The Lapidary Journal
Box 80937
San Diego, CA 92138

INDEX

CORE COLLECTION 2013